Visiting American caves,
917.309 SLO

305930000&

Sloane, Howard N
Jenkintown   09018

WITHDRAWN

Y0-AGA-997

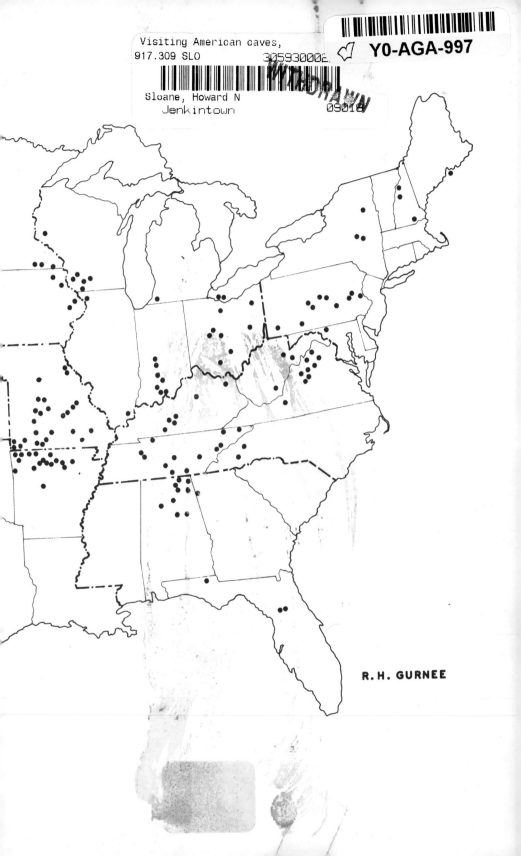

R. H. GURNEE

VISITING
AMERICAN
CAVES

Also by Howard N. Sloane
(with Charles E. Mohr)

CELEBRATED AMERICAN CAVES

Also by Russell H. Gurnee
(with Charles E. Mohr)

CAVE LIFE

VISITING
AMERICAN
CAVES

by Howard N. Sloane
and Russell H. Gurnee

Endorsed by The National Speleological Society

BONANZA BOOKS · NEW YORK

ACKNOWLEDGMENTS

917.309
S/o

Our first acknowledgment is to the National Speleological Society, an organization devoted to the study, exploration, and conservation of caves. Many of the owners, managers, and employees of the caves listed in this book are members of this organization, and the care and custody of their caves are in accordance with the precepts set forth by the Society—that caves are unique and are to be protected. Many members of the Society were consulted in compiling the information for this book, and the files of the National Speleological Society were useful in obtaining data regarding some of the caves.

We should like to express our appreciation specifically to William Varnedoe, Jr. for his information on the caves of the South Atlantic States; to Dr. William Halliday for the caves of the West; to James Schermerhorn for the caves of Arkansas; to Jack Herschend for the caves of Missouri; to Jack Burch for the caves of Texas; to Dr. William White for geological review of the manuscript; and to Richard Anderson for making the files of the N.S.S. available.

The courtesies shown us by the cave owners, personnel of state parks, and the members of the National Park Service were invaluable in helping us to obtain photographs and current information.

Our thanks are also due to Herbert Michelman and Brandt Aymar of Crown Publishers, Inc., to Shirley Robbins and to Susan Gurnee.

We should like to express special appreciation for the patience and hard work of Lucille Sloane and Jeanne Gurnee. Without their cooperation this book would not have been written.

© MCMLXVI by Howard N. Sloane and Russell H. Gurnee
Library of Congress Catalog Card Number: 66-18457
Printed in the United States of America

This edition published by Bonanza Books,
a division of Crown Publishers, Inc.,
a   b   c   d   e   f   g   h

TABLE OF CONTENTS

INTRODUCTION

Caves are not rare. In the United States, according to the records of the National Speleological Society, there are over 12,000 caves that have been discovered and reported. It is estimated that there are over 50,000 caves still to be discovered. Caves are unique, however. They contain an environment unlike anything found on the surface. Fortunately, many of the most beautiful and unusual are protected and displayed for the traveler to see. These include commercial caves owned by individuals, and caves open to the public and controlled by federal or other governmental agencies. This protection ensures to future generations the opportunity to see the caves and their formations in all their beauty and variety. Too often, vandalism mars a cavern scene, causing damage that will take hundreds of centuries to repair.

People in the United States have enjoyed visits to commercial caves since early in the nineteenth century. Caves in Virginia, Kentucky, and Tennessee were open in 1825, when guides with lanterns, lamps, and torches led groups through various corridors and rooms. At that time trails and pathways were only superficially graded, and a special costume was required by the hardy visitors who braved the experience of crawling, crouching, ducking, and scrambling through the sometimes low and narrow passageways. Among the customary hazards of such a trip were singed hair and clothes covered with candle wax.

Early visitors discovered that a uniform temperature exists within a cave and that this, together with pollen-free conditions and an odor-free environment, was exhilarating and produced a feeling of well-being. People seemed capable of activity within the cave that was impossible outside. This idea that the air within caves had some therapeutic value was so strong that it encouraged experiments with patients with respiratory diseases, who were quartered in sections of Mammoth Cave, Kentucky, in stone houses as part of a "cure." In the light of present knowledge, it seems inconceivable that such an experience could result in benefit to people so afflicted.

Today, caves that are open to the public are generally lighted and usually have guide service. Over 200 public caves in the country provide the opportunity to visit the world beneath our feet. In many instances extensive and costly alterations have been necessary to make the cave easily accessible, so that within the short span of an hour you can be introduced to an experience unlike anything else in nature. Here, under the earth, on graded trails and along guided ways, artificial light reveals the beauty of naturally decorated halls and corridors. Dripping water, sparkling crystals, and water-worn walls present a changing diorama of which you become a part. At each turn a new view is seen, and with each step a different perspective appears before your eyes.

Because this experience arouses the curiosity and interest of the explorer in each of us, this guidebook to the tourist caves of the United States has been prepared to permit you to include in your itinerary an adventure that will be of benefit and interest to the whole family.

To give a detailed description of each cave in this volume would not be practical. No description can replace the experience of actually seeing. Each person will react differently to what he sees. We have attempted only to provide some practical information for each cave, together with a little historical background. In this way you can plan your trip to include whatever seems most convenient and most interesting to you.

In order to acquaint you with the many types of formations you will see underground, we have prepared illustrated sections describing individual kinds of speleothems, or cave formations.

If your visit to one or several of the caves listed creates a desire for more information about caves, we have provided a section called "Related Reading." If your visit arouses a yen to explore wild caves, we urge you to get in touch with the National Speleological Society, 2318 North Kenmore Street, Arlington, Virginia. Their office will let you know which of the Society's chapters, or grottoes, is nearest you. They will welcome your interest; and you may find that your casual inquiry will develop into a rewarding hobby. In October, 1965, The National Caves Association, a nationwide organization of commercial cave operators, was formed by a group of responsible cave owners. All of the members of this group are known favorably by the authors, and this association should function as an excellent liaison between the public and commercial caves. It is suggested that those wishing information concerning commercial caves contact the temporary office of the group at The National Caves Association, Marvel Cave Park, Branson, Missouri 65616, area code 417-334-2156.

HOW TO USE THIS TOURIST GUIDE

Every effort has been made to include all caves open to the touring public, including privately owned tourist caves and those operated by the federal government or state, county, and local agencies. The criterion used for inclusion in this directory is whether a family group could get out of its car and enter the cave under supervision without the necessity for elaborate equipment or change of clothing— except for the use of sweaters or warm jackets. This criterion includes caves charging a fee and those having no charge.

Information was obtained from the authors' own lists, from cave owners and operators, and from many members of the National Speleological Society. The information and details were obtained by personal visits and by questionnaires sent to all caves. Verification was obtained wherever possible, but much of the information was culled from the questionnaires and brochures furnished by the caves themselves. Rates, hours open, and so on, are, of course, subject to change without notice.

Every attempt has been made to include all caves meeting the criteria given above, and the authors would appreciate any additions or changes for inclusion in later editions.

All cave custodians will be pleased to send inquirers a brochure containing more details about their caves than can be included in this volume.

Regions

The United States has been divided into 9 regions, as shown on the general map of the country (see endpapers). Individual regions are shown on more detailed maps, and the regions are further divided into the individual states within that area. Consult the Table of Contents for pages of regional maps.

States

Caves within each state are listed in alphabetical order, and may be located on the regional map.

Cave Names

Each cave is listed under the name by which it is best known. For national parks or monuments, if the cave is the main feature of the park, the listing appears under the cave name rather than the park name. Where the cave is merely one feature among many others, the name of the park or monument appears first. An example might be Painted Cave in Bandelier National Monument. This is listed under Bandelier.

Some caves, either of minor importance or on which information was lacking, can be found in the Supplement just preceding the Index.

Many caves have been known by other names. These can be found in the Index at the back of the book.

Road Directions

In visiting the caves, be sure to follow the road directions given below the cave name rather than the address that follows the name. In many instances these addresses are offices for mailing purposes only.

Group Rates

Wherever group rates are mentioned, it is understood that these are organized groups such as the Boy Scouts and Girl Scouts, church groups, educational groups, and so on, and not those formed at the time of the tour.

Parking

All caves have parking and rest-room facilities.

Photography

Most caves carry film for sale and welcome photographers. Some caves have special lighting for photographers.

Lighting

All caves are lighted unless otherwise noted; and in such cases, lighting instructions are given.

Nearby Facilities and Attractions

"Nearby facilities" are usually adjacent to or within a few miles of the cave. The term "all facilities," refers to restaurants, snack bars, gift shops, camping, motels, hotels, cabins, and trailer camps. It does not necessarily include swimming, picnicking, nature trails, and so on. "Nearby attractions" are within a 30-mile radius of the cave.

Closed Caves

Readers who do not find a specific cave in the Regional descriptions are referred to the Index on page (239). The names of commercial caves that have been closed, caves on which no information was obtainable, or caves that may be opened in the future, appear in the Index with an asterisk (*) in place of the page number. In such cases it can be assumed that the caves so shown are not open to the public at this time.

Temperature

Cave temperatures are remarkably uniform. Summer and winter temperatures in the northern part of the country range between 50° F. and 56° F.; in the southern part of the country they range from 56° F. to 69° F. Caves in higher altitudes are usually colder.

Clothing

A light sweater is recommended for the ladies and a jacket for the men. The activity of the cave tour generally prevents any discomfort due to temperature differences. Most caves provide an invigorating environment that enhances the enjoyment and appreciation of the trip.

National Parks or Monuments

Entrance fees are collected under the provisions of the Land and Water Conservation Fund Act of 1965. The Recreation/Conservation card will admit the driver and passengers of a private automobile. Alternative daily and seasonal permits on a per-person basis may be purchased. Fees are not charged for children under 16 years of age.

Types of Caves

An illustrated section beginning on page 1 is intended to acquaint you with the many different types of caves you will see in your travels. This information will help you to appreciate your visit.

Formations

Virtually every cave has formations of one kind or another. Descriptions and illustrations of typical cave formations appear in the section on Cave Formations. Elementary information on how these were formed is included. By reading this section, you will be able to identify most formations when you visit a cave.

Safety Precautions

In the text and supplement are many caves in state-park and other public areas that are listed as "Self-guided." A word of caution is advisable to the uninitiated in visiting nonlighted caves where you must be your own guide. Many of these require physical stamina, and can be dangerous to those not familiar with caving techniques. Under no conditions should a cave that goes beyond daylight be visited without adequate provisions for light. In all cases spare lights should also be carried. If one becomes lost or if his lights fail in a cave, the best procedure is to remain in one spot. It is advisable that at least three persons form a minimum party so that one can go for help, if necessary, without leaving an injured person alone. This also minimizes the possibility of light failure. Hard hats are advisable to prevent head injuries. Chocolate candy or other sustaining food, such as raisins, might well be carried in case of emergency. Heavy high shoes and warm clothing are essential. Always notify someone in attendance on the outside when you enter a cave and when you expect to return. These minimum precautions may prevent serious injury and even loss of life.

TYPES OF CAVES

LIMESTONE CAVES

Limestone is a sedimentary rock that was originally formed at the bottom of ancient seas. Hundreds of millions of years were needed to accumulate the deposits of marine life, shells, skeletons, and coral and compress them into stone and thrust them above the sea, creating the huge limestone regions of the world. Formed by this gradual deposition of many ingredients, including billions of tiny sea creatures, limestones have many different hues, textures, and degrees of purity. A common feature of these rocks is their tendency to be dissolved by rainwater, especially after the water has percolated through acid vegetable matter in the soil. This acid condition causes erosion of the rock, and in some instances so dissolves it as to cause caverns beneath the surface. Such caverns range from tiny cracks and tubes, which conduct water to lower levels, to gigantic tunnels and chambers. Nearly 95 percent of the world's caves are found in limestone.

Caves in limestone are, geologically speaking, relatively young. The very factors that are needed to make a cave—solution and erosion—are also the factors that destroy it. It is possible to compare some aspects of the "life cycle" of a cave with those of the animal kingdom. Birth, which took place millions of years ago during mountain-building processes, bends, twists, and fractures the limestone that is the matrix for the cave. Childhood occurs when the thousands of cracks and crevices carry the aggressive rainwater through the limestone, in search of the water table. Some of these fractures capture more water than others, and as soon as a few begin to dominate, the drainage becomes greater and greater. In youth, the cave is a barren tunnel partially or completely filled with water. Maturity is reached when the water is drained away and dripping water from the land above penetrates the ceiling and forms glistening decorations. All is wet and gleaming. Old age is reached when the

Courtesy of Carlsbad Caverns, New Mexico. National Park Service photo.

atmosphere becomes dry and the formations begin to turn to dust and powder. The cover over the cave has become so thin that there is danger of collapse. Finally in death the ceiling of the cave falls, leaving only a sinkhole, gorge, or valley to mark the site.

Each of these stages takes hundreds of thousands of years. All these conditions can be found in the caves of the United States, but most of the caves listed in this book are those at the peak of their beauty and appeal.

SANDSTONE CAVES AND CLIFF DWELLINGS

Sandstone is one of the most common sedimentary rocks. It is so easily eroded by weather and wind that the face of sandstone cliffs is often pitted with shallow holes and pockets. Meandering rivers scoop out great hollows and leave huge overhangs in the sharp bends of a gorge. Sometimes these hollows tunnel completely through the wall to form the arches and natural bridges that are so picturesque in the rimrock country of the western United States.

Such shallow caves were very valuable to the early settlers of the West. Indian cultures developed within the shelter of these caves, and protection from weather and enemy attack encouraged the building of permanent settlements. Large cliff houses were made of clay and straw, and elaborate systems of ladders and stairways enabled the early Indians to reach the numerous rooms.

Because the arid climate has preserved these remains in remarkable condition, they can be seen today in their natural state in some national parks and monuments.

While some of these shelters do not extend beyond the sight of natural light, they are true caves, and therefore have been included in this book.

Sandstone Cave, New Mexico. Photo by Russell H. Gurnee.

SEA CAVES

Water, wind, and sand are powerful grinding agents that will scour and destroy the hardest rock. The coastline of our country has been pounded by surging seas for hundreds of thousands of years. Broad beaches and rolling dunes shift and change with the wind and tide. Towering cliffs hold back the sea, retreating slowly under the relentless hammering of the surf. Water, seeking out the weakest part of the cliff, grinds and chews away at the rock until it has burrowed into the face of the cliff, booming and spraying against the little hollow until it has collapsed the wall. Occasionally a joint in the rock will permit the water to enter deeper and deeper until a tunnel is cut out—a chamber filled with the thundering surge of the waves and the groaning compression of air.

This is the way most sea caves are formed, and the stone might be of any material. Because the action is principally one of abrasion, in time the hardest granite or the softest chalk may be cut away by the action of the waves.

Courtesy of Sea Lion Caves, Oregon.

Courtesy of Alabaster Caverns, Oklahoma. Photograph by J. H. Schermerhorn.

GYPSUM CAVES

Gypsum is best known to us in a dehydrated form used as the chief ingredient in wallboard for construction in our homes. Gypsum originally occurs as natural stone, and has many economic uses. It is quite common throughout the world. Gypsum, however, is also soluble, and can be cavernous, although it rarely permits the formation of caves of the size found in limestone.

Traces of gypsum appear in limestone caves, usually as secondary formations and wall decorations, and sometimes in the clay of the floor in the form of crystals and needles. Major caves entirely in gypsum are quite rare, however, and are usually found in arid regions of the American southwest.

Gypsum rock is easily scratched—sometimes even with a fingernail. Alabaster, a form of gypsum which has been used for thousands of years in statuary and carved utensils, is also found in caves.

ICE CAVES

There are many ice caves in the United States, but only a few are in areas that are accessible to the tourist. These caves are usually found at high elevations and in regions where the mean annual temperature is at or below freezing.

Ice caves are actually natural storage areas for the cold air of winter. The rock

4

covering of the cave acts as an insulation against the sun and summer air. The duration of the summer in ice-cave areas is not long enough for the temperature to rise above freezing. The result is that each winter and spring more cold air and water replenish the ice perpetually stored within the cave.

Before the days of modern refrigeration, caves with ice were used to provide the luxury of cold drinks in the hottest days of summer. In Italy, noblemen sent runners to the ice caves in the mountains to bring ice for the banquets and dinner tables of Rome.

Some of the lava tubes in the western United States have large quantities of ice that have formed in the freezing air of the cave. Some of these deposits are thousands of years old. Many of the more delicate formations melt in the fall of the year, but they are replaced in the spring as the melting water from the surface drips into the freezing air of the cave.

Crystal-clear icicles and prismatic shapes glisten on the walls of some ice caves. Some of the frost crystals are so delicate that the presence of a person in the room will cause them to melt and shatter. Dripping water causes knobby ice stalagmites and slippery, sloping floors. All the beauty of a winter scene is revealed in the blue-and-white galleries of an ice cave.

Courtesy of Crystal Ice Cave, Idaho.

BOULDER CAVES

Occasionally caves will be formed by the collapse of a cliff face—the debris piling up at the bottom leaving covered rooms and passages between the rocks. Generally, when formed, these rooms and crevices are quite small and narrow. In several instances, however, glaciers have carried debris against a cliff face, fracturing off large sections of the wall. With the melting of the ice, the boulders are gently lowered to the base of the cliff. This action leaves strange balanced rocks, broad roof spans, and passages in among the rocks.

These caves, usually small, are curious, and of interest mainly to geologists.

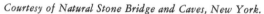

Courtesy of Natural Stone Bridge and Caves, New York.

HISTORICAL CAVES

Man's relationship to caves stretches back into the dim past of prehistory. The earliest permanent home of early man was in the shelter of rock overhangs and the entrances of natural caves. The remains and evidences of generations of early people are valuable records of their lives and times. Fortunately, the nature of caves and their protective ability have preserved these remains, which might otherwise have been lost forever.

Many historical caves and archaeological sites in this country are protected in national parks and monuments and state preserves that range from Russell Cave in Alabama, where archaeologists have found evidences of Indian occupation dating back 9,000 years, to numerous southern caves that contain remains of Civil War saltpeter mining only one hundred years ago.

Many of the historical sites described in this book are shelters used by the

*Cliff dwellings, courtesy of Montezuma Castle National Monument, Arizona.
National Park Service photo.*

"cliff-dwelling" Pueblo Indians of the West. Most are national monuments. The early Indians developed a high culture, using the limited means at hand to overcome the natural hazards of a hostile land. By gradual adaptation, their shelters became elaborate "apartment houses" that were continuously occupied for hundreds of years.

The desert air and sheltering rock have preserved these dwellings, and with them many fragile artifacts. From these we are able to piece together the story of the lives of early occupants.

Mammoth Cave, Kentucky, courtesy of National Park Concessions, Inc. Photo by W. Ray Scott.

LAVA TUBES

Most caves take hundreds of thousands of years to form, but nature, in a capricious mood, sometimes bypasses this time problem with the energy and power released by volcanoes. Volcanic eruptions spew forth millions of tons of molten rock in great spasms that can change the face of the earth. These flows of liquid stone surge like rivers down the slopes of the cones and spread out around the base of the volcano like frosting from a cake. The flows occur in a remarkably short period of time, with the great walls of scalding stone sometimes advancing as fast as a man can walk. As the flow spreads out on the level land at the base of the cone, and its rate slackens, the surface of the lava begins to "freeze" and become a solid. Since the core is still hot and liquid, the center continues to flow out the end of this now crudely formed tube. If the conditions are just right for the flow to continue, the snakelike path of this molten river will sometimes extend for several miles. In a very short time the core of the tube will drain out the end, and the entire flow will cool, leaving a tunnel.

In this cooling process, tiny stalactites of liquid stone form on the ceiling, almost in an instant, adding decoration to these otherwise barren, subway-like tunnels.

This is the extent of the growth of a lava tube. Born in the fiery flash of the flaming lava, maturing in the moments of the draining of the tube, it remains in a suspended state until the roof collapses or until it is filled again by later lava flows.

Courtesy of Lava Beds National Monument, California. National Park Service photo.

CAVE FORMATIONS

STALACTITES

"Oozing out in drops" is the definition of this Greek word that describes the icicle-like formations found in caves the world over.

Each stalactite begins its life as a single drop of water that forms, swells, quivers, then drops to the floor below. The subsequent drops continue in seemingly endless fashion. If the water is pure and free of minerals, nothing occurs but the patter and splatter of the steady drip. However, if the water becomes saturated with calcium carbonate from the limestone layer above the cave, each drop will leave a tiny deposit of this calcite as it leaves the ceiling.

First a tiny ring just the size of the drop is formed; then ring forms upon ring until a slender, drop-sized tube hangs from the ceiling. The formation might continue to grow in this shape until it reaches the floor. These slender "soda straws" sometimes grow to be 10 feet long—often as a single crystal. This condition is unusual, however, as ordinarily the tiny hole through the center of the tube will not carry the water from the source above, causing the water to flow down the outside of the straw, adding to its deposit and creating the familiar carrot or icicle shape.

Some stalactites grow to gigantic proportions limited only by the height of the room and the stability of the joint that supplies it with more calcite for its growth.

The simple ingredients in a drop of water, a tiny bit of mineral matter, the relentless pull of gravity, and centuries of time all work together to create these beautiful natural scenes beneath the earth.

Courtesy of Ohio Caverns, Ohio.

STALAGMITES

Every drop of water that falls in a cave must, of course, land somewhere. It can drop in a pool or stream or on a sloping wall, mudbank, or fallen stone. If it falls in water, it ripples and is gone. If it splatters on a steeply sloping wall, it fans out and flows down as part of a sheet of water. As in the development of a stalactite, this action will cause the deposit of calcite; and if dripping continues for thousands of years, the wall will be covered with a solid coating called "flowstone."

If the drop falls on a flat, solid surface, the violent action of the water will concentrate the loss of calcite on a spot usually directly beneath its parent stalactite, and a tiny mound will form—the birth of a stalagmite. The rate of flow of water, the distance the drop has to fall, and its impurities are only a few of the factors that determine the characteristics of this budding formation.

A stalagmite is generally rounder and smoother than a stalactite, and has no central tube as its parent does. It may assume a bizarre shape or it may grow to be perfectly straight to a height of 10 feet or more. These straight formations are called "broomsticks," which sometimes have a diameter no larger than that of a silver dollar. If the stalagmite, continuing to build and grow, reaches the stalactite above, the two may join to form a solid pillar of stone reaching from floor to ceiling. This is called a "column." If the ceiling is of great height, and the water splatters over a large area, a stubby, flat, dinner-plate formation will occur that resembles a stack of pancakes.

All these formations are incredibly old. A tiny nub of stalagmite may have started its growth long before the great pyramids of Egypt were built. A huge column may have begun to form when man was still living in the caves of Europe.

Flowstone, courtesy of Cathedral Caverns, Alabama.

Stalagmite, courtesy of Tuckaleechee Caverns, Tennessee.

Columns, courtesy of Ohio Caverns, Ohio.

HELICTITES

Perhaps no other cave formation has proved more puzzling to both visitor and scientist than the bizarre erratics knows as "helictites." These strange formations defy gravity, and twist and turn in their growth like tree roots in search of water. There were as many theories as experts among early explorers; thus the various solutions to the strange behavior of these beautiful "stone roots" ranged from wind currents to earth tremors.

A helictite starts its growth as a tiny stalactite—a single drop that leaves a tiny ring of calcite on the wall or ceiling as it drops to the floor. It may continue as a tiny soda straw for many years, straight and true. Then for some unknown reason the chemical composition of the water changes slightly. Some impurities may appear in the water, causing the single crystal structure to change from a cylindrical, prismatic shape to a slightly conical one—each cone crystal fitting into the previous one like an inverted stack of ice-cream cones. This shape is very unstable. As the crystals grow, the direction of the end of the straw might wander from the vertical just as the stack of ice-cream cones might sway or bend. Since this, as well as every hanging formation, has a tiny tube running through it, water will continue to flow through this tube until it emerges as a drop regardless of the direction the tube takes. The result of this wandering can cause some of the most curious and often beautiful formations to be found in caves.

There are many questions still to be answered—many examples that seem to prove the experts wrong. No one knows why one little soda straw hanging in a cluster of its fellows will have a corkscrew twist to the end while all the others are straight; or why some huge stalactites will cease to grow as normal carrot-shaped formations, while small helictites sprout out of the sides like fishhooks and rootlets.

Perhaps one day we shall know the trigger that sets off these strange antics of helictites, but that knowledge is not necessary to appreciate the sight of these delicate bits of twisting stone, perhaps the most beautiful of all cave formations.

Helictites, courtesy of Caverns of Sonora, Texas.

Helictites, courtesy of Lehman Caves National Monument, Nevada. National Park Service photo.

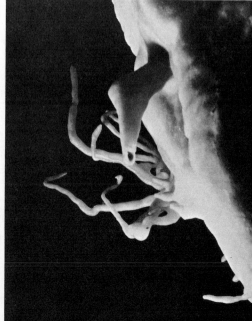

RIMSTONE POOLS

The crystal-clear water that drips, flows, and forms pools in many caves is actually highly saturated with minerals picked up as the water flows through the limestone rock that covers the cave.

These minerals do not dull the brilliance of the pools, but they do trouble those housewives who have to contend with the "hard" water of limestone country. Lime deposits in cooking utensils and "scum" in wash water are caused by this saturation of minerals.

There is a bright side, for this very saturation makes possible the magnificent displays of flowstone formations found in caves. Stalactites, stalagmites, columns, shields, and flowstone are merely the residue of this mineral matter transported by water and deposited in bizarre and fanciful shapes.

Usually, when this saturated water flows slowly through a rock-lined channel, its impurities are in equilibrium with its carbon dioxide content. If, however, any disturbance in the stream channel causes the water to ripple or foam, this balance is upset, causing a tiny bit of carbon dioxide to turn into gas (just as bubbles are released when a soda bottle is opened). Some of the calcite is deposited in order to permit the water to return to a state of equilibrium. The water flows on as the deposit of calcite continues for perhaps thousands of years until it actually dams up the stream. These dams impound what are known as "rimstone pools," and are perfectly level, controlled in height by the continued growth of the deposit. In the same manner as beavers dam up a stream, by plugging the holes with clay and sticks, the mineral in the water raises the level of the dam, where the ripples and foam form as the water flows over the top edge.

In some caves, huge dams 100 feet across have impounded thousands of gallons of water; but usually the dams that make rimstone pools are only a few feet across or on sloping surfaces a few inches long. These limpid pools, like terraced fields of rice paddies, gracefully lower the water in ladder-like steps to the continuing stream below.

Courtesy of Massanutten Caverns, Virginia.

FOSSILS

Limestone, being the deposit of millions upon millions of ancient sea creatures and debris, sometimes captured the remains of these sea animals intact. Many kinds of seashells, clams, and coral were entombed in this sedimentary rock, and the outlines of their form and shape have been preserved in the solid stone. Many of these creatures were destroyed during the formation of the stone, but some of their forms were replaced with minerals, and so became harder than the surrounding rock.

Most caves occur in limestone rock, and often fossils may be seen projecting from the walls and ceilings. One common fossil found in the United States is the stem of a sea plant called a crinoid. This plant grew in shallow seas. It was attached to the bottom by a root, and had a long, snakelike stem that reached to the surface, not unlike the present water plants, and terminated in a flower. Some of these plants were 60 feet long; and the stems, which are most often preserved, are a series of doughnut rings joined together in a continuous tube. They are so common that the early Indians strung them through the hole in the center and used them as beads.

Bones of extinct animals (much later in geologic time than the seashell) are also found in caves. These bones were deposited after the cave formed, and might be the remains of trapped animals that fell into the cave; or debris left by predators who dragged their prey into the caves; or deposits washed into the cave by streams or rain.

Sea-worm trails, courtesy of Wonder Cave, Texas.

Crinoids, courtesy of Jewel Cave, Tennessee.

GYPSUM FLOWERS, SELENITE NEEDLES, AND ANTHODITES

Some of the most unusual formations found beneath the earth are also the most beautiful. In certain dry areas of some caves, gypsum will form on the walls and make a crust that sparkles and glistens in the light of the lamp. In some cases tiny patches will seem to sprout out into beautiful, graceful stone flowers that appear to be extruded from the wall. It is not unusual to find twists and curls that project 10 to 12 inches without any support. These gypsum flowers are extremely fragile, and will sometimes fall of their own weight.

In the same general areas that support gypsum flowers, crystals are sometimes found that seem to form in the moist air of the cave. Selenite needles apparently form from a seed crystal on the floor, and then, seemingly unattached to anything, grow as a single straw sometimes to 2½ feet in length. These needles occur in piles on the floor like jackstraws, completely unattached and loose.

Anthodites are often described as the stone flowers of the caves, and they certainly have the delicate and fragile appearance that would give them that name. Hairlike crystals radiate from a central point, making little blooms of crystals on the wall or ceiling. As are most speleothems, anthodites are also composed of calcium carbonate, but the calcium carbonate is in a different crystal form. This other form is the mineral aragonite. It is the different growth behavior of aragonite that gives the anthodite its unique shape.

Gypsum flowers.
Photo by
Russell H. Gurnee.

Selenite needles, courtesy of
Cumberland Caverns, Tennessee.
Photo by Russell H. Gurnee.

Anthodite flowers,
courtesy of Skyline Caverns,
Virginia.

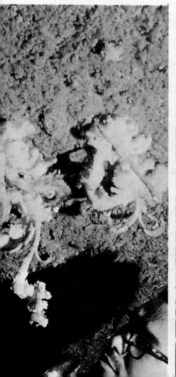

SHIELDS

Curiously round and flat formations occasionally found in limestone caves are known as "shields" or "palettes." These disk-shaped layers of calcite project from the walls and ceilings (and occasionally floors) of rooms and passageways. The actual formation of these objects could be shown in a cutaway section revealing two flat disks sandwiched together. Water flows between these two plates—which do not adhere—and at some time during the growth process, stalactites begin to form along the edge. The question of why these disks form, why they do not cement themselves together, and how they can form at different angles to the bedding and joints of the parent limestone have conflicting answers.

One thing seems to be sure. They are found only in certain caves and in certain areas. It is possible that either the limestone matrix or impurities in the stone above the cave influence the growth of these beautiful decorations, which sometimes reach 10 feet in diameter. It is also possible that minute earth movements and hydrostatic pressure play a part in their growth.

Courtesy of Grand Caverns, Virginia. Virginia State Chamber of Commerce photo.

BOXWORK

In the formation of mountains and continents, tremendous forces are at work that will bend, twist, and shatter the hardest stone, and fracture the most massive rock. Limestone, forming in huge sheets and layers, is very vulnerable to fracture. Any warping or twisting of the beds sends cracks and joints through the layers, sometimes for many miles. Severe pressures often fracture the stone into small checkerboard-like layers so porous that water will stand in, or flow through this maze as it would through gravel. Since there is no major conduit for the water to select, all the joints tend to fill uniformly with calcite carried in the water. These cracks eventually become completely filled with veins of calcite. Further growth is not possible once all the cracks are cemented together. The fractured layer then becomes whole again.

If other conditions are then just right for the formation of a cave in that area, the solution of the rock may take place, leaving little ribbons of calcite projecting from the walls and ceiling. Some of these ribbons are so thin that they are translucent, yet they are hard enough to withstand the solution of the limestone matrix that gave them their shape.

Courtesy of Wind Cave National Park, South Dakota. National Park Service photo.

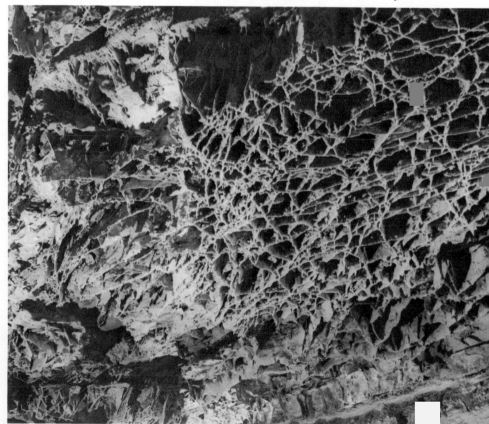

CAVE PEARLS

Cave pearls are rare and exotic formations. They are often overlooked, and inadvertently become trodden underfoot in the dim light of a "wild" cave or destroyed by the trail builder in a commercial cave. Disguised as water-worn pebbles in a pool, they sometimes escape the scrutiny of visitor and guide alike. Occasionally they are found in an ideal setting, where they glisten and turn in their "nest" as the water splatters from the ceiling.

Cave pearls, technically called "oolites," are formed by the deposit of calcite (dissolved limestone) on a tiny bit of sand or a pebble. This same material forms stalactites and stalagmites and covers the floor with a pavement of "frozen stone." However, one element is required in the growth of a cave pearl that is missing in the growth of all other cave formations. That element is movement—the motion of the particle that serves as a nucleus for the pearl and causes the deposit of material to form in uniform layers around the "seed."

Most cave pearls form in a shallow pool beneath a steady flow of water. This constantly running waterfall causes the sand and gravel to be suspended by the turbulence of the water. The agitation causes some of the calcite held in the water to deposit on the minute bits of sand, until they are covered with the material and look like tiny beads. After many years of this growth, they sink to the bottom from their own weight. If the pool is shallow enough, the running water will still turn these little spheres so that they continue to grow until they finally get so heavy that they adhere to the bottom and become part of the pool.

During this growth period the pearls are perfectly free and separated from the stone floor. They are suspended on a film of water that permits them to rotate endlessly round and round, sometimes forming perfect spheres or even tiny pointed tops that fit into tapered holes in the floor. Most cave pearls are smaller than marbles, but occasionally they grow to the size of softballs.

Unfortunately, like most cave formations, these pearls have no value out of their environment because they must remain wet to retain their luster. (They will dry out and turn to powder when taken from the cave.) Their real beauty and rarity are in the place of their birth where the ceaseless splattering of the water and the sparkling drops need only the light of the lamp to reveal their beauty.

Courtesy of Carlsbad Caverns, New Mexico. National Park Service photo.

POPCORN, LILY PADS, AND DOGTOOTH SPAR

Under certain conditions in highly saturated atmospheres within a cave room, curious grapelike clusters not unlike popcorn form on the walls, formations, and even the floor and ceiling. The presence of clear, still pools in these rooms leads to speculation that these speleothems might form beneath the water. It is generally accepted, however, that popcorn forms in the air and that the apparent stratification of the line of growth is due to stratification of the saturated air within the room.

The waterline of some pools might be emphasized by a thin layer of calcite that forms at right angles to the sides, and projects out into the pool. These flat projections sometimes reach large proportions, and are called popularly "lily pads."

Occasionally in rooms that are completely submerged, the floor, walls, and ceiling will be covered with crystals of calcite. Under completely submerged conditions, the crystals are free to develop their natural scalenohedral shape. These angular crystals, called "dogtooth spar," sometimes grow to be 4 or 5 inches long, and project from the walls and ceilings. They vary in color from white to pale yellow and orange to onyx.

*Popcorn, courtesy of
Meramec Caverns, Missouri.*

*Dogtooth spar, courtesy of
Sitting Bull Crystal Caverns,
South Dakota.*

Lily pads, courtesy of Onondaga Cave, Missouri.

MOON MILK

One of the strangest cave formations is the semiliquid, cheeselike material popularly called "moon milk." This secondary formation is seen on the floors, walls, and ceilings of certain caves; and while it is similar in many ways to other deposits, it is unique in that it does not harden or turn to stone.

Analysis of this material shows it can be any of several minerals, but theories as to its origin are mixed. It is possible that the formation of this material is by biological means rather than chemical—bacterial action capable of breaking down the stone to this semiliquid state. This mystery is further compounded by the discovery of this material as a dry powder and a granular snow in certain parts of some caves.

This is not a major point of interest in your visit to one of the tourist caves of the country, but it points up one of the many unanswered questions that occur in these natural underground laboratories.

Cumberland Caverns, Tennessee. Photo by Russell H. Gurnee.

BREAKDOWN

Old age and decay do not attack an entire cave at once. They creep up on it bit by bit as surface valleys cut down into the limestone. Cave passages often end against heaps of fallen limestone blocks at the intersection of the passage with a hillside. These fallen blocks are termed "breakdown."

Breakdown blocks are seen in most caves. They vary in size from pebbles to chunks the size of a house. The piles of breakdown may be only a few scattered fragments or may take the form of breakdown mountains sometimes 100 feet high over which the tourist trail climbs in a series of switchbacks.

There are many processes that trigger breakdown, but most of them occur either very early in the history of the cave or very late. Rockfall is very rare during the mature years of the cave; and it is during the mature years that caves are seen by visitors. Dry cave passages with their naturally arched roofs, and without the influence of man-made stresses from drilling and blasting, are remarkably stable structures. While you may look with awe at the mountain of rubble that fell thousands of years ago when the present landscape was formed, you need not glance apprehensively at the ceiling.

CAVE FILLS

All the speleothems you will see in the caves have been deposited by some sort of chemical reaction after the cavern itself was formed. Less attractive, perhaps, but equally important are the cave fillings that have been deposited by the mechanical action of water. These are the layers of sand, silt, and clay that cover the floors of most caves.

In many commercial caves, trails for the visitors have been prepared by making trenches up to 6 feet deep in the cave fills. As you walk comfortably through these miniature road cuts (in a passage the early explorers traversed flat on their stomachs), the fills can be seen in cross section. They are layered like surface rocks; and each layer may be different in color and texture from the ones above and below it. These strata of loose sand and clay record the story of the water that passed through the cave in its youth. Coarse gravels may mean rough, fast-moving streams; fine clay and mud may have been deposited by slowly percolating water with perceptible current. In reading the riddle of the cave's early history, the scientist finds more clues locked in the unattractive fills than in the glistening stalactites.

The fills also serve as containers for minerals and graves for animals. Gypsum crystals grow in the fills of some caves. The crystals of saltpeter, mined in many southern Appalachian caves in the early nineteenth century, occur almost exclusively in the fills. And graves? Animals sometimes fall into caves through pits and sinkholes, or crawl into the caves to die. Skeletons of animals thousands of years old are fairly frequently found buried in the cavern fills.

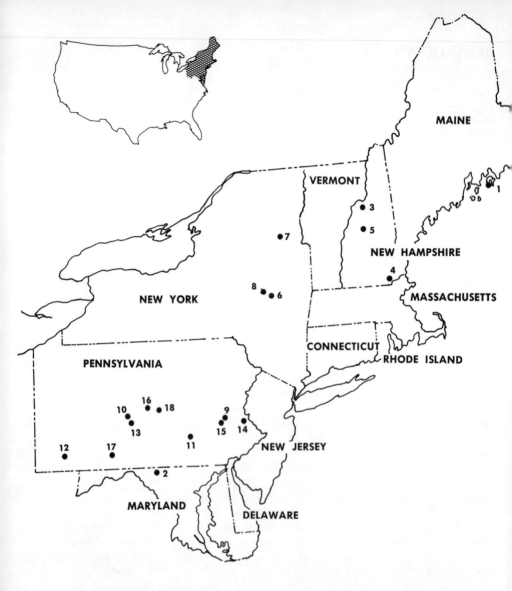

1. Anemone Cave, Maine
2. Crystal Grottoes, Maryland
3. Lost River, New Hampshire
4. Mystery Hill Caves, New Hampshire
5. Polar Caves, New Hampshire
6. Howe Caverns, New York
7. Natural Stone Bridge and Caves, New York
8. Secret Caverns, New York
9. Crystal Cave, Pennsylvania
10. Indian Caverns, Pennsylvania
11. Indian Echo Caverns, Pennsylvania
12. Laurel Caverns, Pennsylvania
13. Lincoln Caverns, Pennsylvania
14. Lost River Caverns, Pennsylvania
15. Onyx Cave, Pennsylvania
16. Penn's Cave, Pennsylvania
17. Wonderland Caverns, Pennsylvania
18. Woodward Cave, Pennsylvania

1. NEW ENGLAND AND NORTH ATLANTIC REGION

Connecticut
Delaware
Maine
Maryland
Massachusetts
New Hampshire
New Jersey
New York
Pennsylvania
Rhode Island
Vermont

Most of the New England region was glaciated—covered with a huge crushing load of ice nearly a mile thick that scraped the surface free of trees and debris and changed the face of the landscape. Caves that might have existed before this invasion were filled with rubble or crushed under the enormous weight of the ice. A few caves, structurally strong enough to withstand this stress, survived and were enlarged by the drain-off of the tremendous flow of water released by the melting ice. Thus a characteristic shape for the caves in limestone in New England might be said to be a sinuous, narrow waterway, joint oriented, and partially filled with the pebbles and debris flushed through the cave after the change in climate. Because the changing climate also limited the growth of secondary formations, the caves of this region are generally not so highly decorated as those of the southern part of the country. Exceptions are found in sections of Pennsylvania. New England has some of the finest examples of boulder caves and sea caves in the United States.

Anemone Cave, Maine. Courtesy of Acadia National Park, Maine.

MAINE

ANEMONE CAVE, Acadia National Park, Bar Harbor. Reached from U.S. Route 1 at Ellsworth onto State Route 3 to Bar Harbor. From Bar Harbor ¾ mile south on the road to Ocean Drive to the Anemone Cave parking area. Phone: 207-228-3338.

Anemone Cave is one of the finest examples of a sea cave. Located on the eastern shoreline of Mount Desert Island in Acadia National Park, it has been carved by sea action for a depth of 82 feet. Below the overhanging roof of the cave is a tidepool containing a great wealth of color and a variety of marine plants and animals. Conspicuous among these are the sea anemones for which the cave is named. Sea urchins, yellow and green sponges, starfish, brittle stars, green crabs, limpets, barnacles, periwinkles, purple rock snails, sea cucumbers, and other sights are easily seen in the clear water.

Visitors should note that the cave is ⅕ of a mile from the parking area along a well-marked trail. The cave is best visited in the morning before ten o'clock while the sunlight lights up the cave's interior. Tide conditions combined with the morning sun offer the best viewing. The most advantageous tide is half tide or lower; at this time one may enter the cave dryshod. The approach to the cave is over rough, rocky terrain that requires care and appropriate footwear.

Open May 1 to December 1 all day.

Rates: no charge.

Self-guided tour: no lights needed.

On premises: camping, trailer camp, picnicking. *Nearby:* restaurant, snack bar, gift shop, motels, hotels, cabins, baby sitters, and all facilities in Bar Harbor.

Nearby attractions: Moose Point State Park, Camden Hills State Park, Acadia National Park, Lamoin State Park, Penobscot Bay, many lakes, fishing, swimming, Maine-coast shore resorts.

MARYLAND

CRYSTAL GROTTOES, Route 1, Boonsboro. On State Route 34, about 1 mile south of U.S. Alternate 40. Phone: 301-432-8203.

Crystal Grottoes is a well-formed cave with many interesting speleothems. The lighting enhances the beauty of the cave. It was discovered in 1920 and commercialized in 1922.

Open April 1 to December 1, 9:30 A.M. to 5:00 P.M. daily.

Guided tour: one hour.

Rates: adults, $1.00; children, $0.60; groups, $0.60 each.

On premises: gift shop, picnicking. *Nearby:* restaurant, camping, motels, hotels, cabins.

Nearby attractions: Seneca Creek State Park, Site of John Brown's Trial, Harpers Ferry National Historic Park, Civil War Showcase, Gathland State Park, Shepherd College, Hood College, Fort Frederick State Park, Fort Tonoloway State Park, St. Mary's College, Mont Alto State Park (Pennsylvania), Gettysburg College (Pennsylvania), Potomac River, Fantasyland Story Book Park (Pennsylvania), Antietam Battlefield, Washington's Monument, Gambrill's State Park, Catactin Recreational Demonstration Area, Cunningham Falls State Park, Barbara Fritchie's Home, Gettysburg National Cemetery and Park (Pennsylvania).

NEW HAMPSHIRE

LOST RIVER, North Woodstock. State Route 112, about 6 miles west of North Woodstock. Phone: 603-745-6192.

Lost River Reservation contains a gorge, caverns, potholes, and Paradise Falls. The cave is formed of large boulders that were pushed down by the glaciers many centuries ago. The boulders have fallen in such a way that it is possible to follow a passageway among them.

Open May 30 through mid-October 9:00 A.M. to 5:00 P.M.

Guided tour: one hour.

Rates: adults, $1.00; children, $0.50.

On premises: snack bar, gift shop, camping, cabins, picnicking. *Nearby:* motel, hotel, cabins.

Nearby attractions: Flume, Cannon Mountain, Chairlift, Kinsman Mountain, Moosilauke Mountain, Franconia Notch State Park, the Great Stone Face, Morse Museum, Polar Caves, Mittersill Ski Area, covered bridge.

Courtesy of Mystery Hill Caves, New Hampshire.

NEW HAMPSHIRE

MYSTERY HILL CAVES, North Salem. On State Route 111, 5 miles northeast of Interstate 93 (Exit 3). Phone: 603-432-2530.

Mystery Hill Caves are perhaps better known locally as Pattee's Caves. In the 1930's Jonathan Pattee excavated these "caves" for the purpose of finding out their archaeological background, and so disturbed the archaeological site that he may have removed all possibility of ever discovering the true history of these unusual structures, which are a series of rock rooms, many with roofs of huge stones. Some are now exposed to the skies. Much has been written about the past history of these "caves," with archaeological claims ranging from theories of ancient Eskimo dwellings, built when the Eskimos were forced south by the Ice Age, to a theory, presented in book form, that the site was inhabited and built by Irish Culdee monks fleeing from Viking raiders in 900 A.D. Note that below the speaking tube on the left is the entrance to the "Abbot's Bed." In the background is the hearth and above it the chimney flue.

Open from April to November, daily in summer and weekends in fall and spring, all from 9:30 A.M. to 6:00 P.M.

Guided tour: 40 to 60 minutes.

Rates: adults, $1.00; children 8 to 12, $0.50; 5 to 7, $0.25; under 5, free; group rates, 15 or more, half price.

On premises: snack bar, gift shop, picnicking, artifact display. *Nearby:* all facilities.

Nearby attractions: Benson's Animal Farm, Canobie Lake Park, Kingston State Park.

NEW HAMPSHIRE

POLAR CAVES, Plymouth. On State Highway 25, about 5 miles west of Interstate 93 (exits 25 and 26). Phone: 603-536-1888.

Polar Caves is an unusual group of massive granite blocks pushed to the base of a cliff by glacial action 14,000 to 20,000 years ago. These have formed an amazing series of caves and passages through which people can walk. Parts of the cave are lighted with "black light" to show fluorescence of the rocks.

Open mid-May to October 12 from 9:00 A.M. to 5:00 P.M. except in July and August, when the time is from 8:30 A.M. to 6:00 P.M.

Guided tour: 45 minutes.

Rates: adults, $1.25; children, $0.50.

On premises: cafeteria, gift shop, picnicking, mineral exhibit, nature trails. *Nearby:* camping, motels, hotels, cabins, trailer camp.

Nearby attractions: Lost River Glacial Caverns, White Mountains Resort Areas, The Flume, Natureland, Clark's Trading Post, Morse Museum, Dartmouth College and Skiway, Cardigan State Park, Wellington State Park, Newfound Lake, Squam Lake, Winnipesaukee Lake.

Courtesy of Howe Caverns, New York.

NEW YORK

HOWE CAVERNS, Howes Cave. On Route 7 between Central Bridge and Cobleskill. Phone: 518-296-8990.

Howe Caverns winds for nearly a mile and a half along the banks of a subterranean stream, 160 to 200 feet below the surface. The last ¼ mile can be seen only by boat, as pictured here, which is optional to visitors. An elevator takes visitors to the cave level.

Open all year, May 1 to September 30, from 8:00 A.M. to 8:00 P.M.; October 1 to April 30, from 9:00 A.M. to 6:00 P.M.

Guided tour: one hour and twenty minutes plus optional boat ride (¼ mile).

Rates: adults, regular tour $1.90, with boat ride, $2.50; children 10 to 14, regular tour, $0.95, with boat ride, $1.25.

On premises: restaurant, snack bar, gift shop, camping, motel, lodge, picnicking. *Nearby:* all facilities.

Nearby attractions: Old Stone Fort, Secret Caverns, Lower Adirondacks, Baseball Hall of Fame (Cooperstown), Schenectady, Fulton Lakes Chain, Sacandaga Lake, Otsego Lake, John Boyd Thacher State Park, New York State Museum, Schuyler Mansion, Cooperstown Indian Museum, James Fenimore Cooper Home, and many other lakes and reservoirs.

Courtesy of Natural Stone Bridge and Caves, New York.

NEW YORK

NATURAL STONE BRIDGE AND CAVES, Pottersville. Off U.S. 9 in Pottersville. Phone: Chestertown, N.Y., 3099.

Natural Stone Bridge and Caves is a series of caves and grottoes, potholes, tunnels, waterfalls and rapids, cliffs and ledges in a woodland setting. There are at least seven caves, including Barrel, Echo, Garnet, Geyser, Kelly Slide, Noisy and Lost Pool. All of them have pools, running streams, or waterfalls in them. The caves are easily traversed by adults or children. A self-guiding tour map is given each visitor to enable him to see the entire area. Many of the caves are now lighted.

Open May through October 8:00 A.M. until dark for tours.
Self-guiding tours: from one hour. Flashlights advisable in some caves.
Rates: adults, $1.50; children 6 to 12, $0.50. Group rates are available for 10 or more.
On premises: snacks and refreshments, two gift shops, picnicking. *Nearby:* restaurants, camping, motels, hotels, cabins, trailer camp, resort areas.
Nearby attractions: Barton's Garnet Mines, Mount Marcy (highest point in New York), Lake Champlain, Schroon Lake, Lake George, Paradox Lake, Crown Point, Ticonderoga, Frontier Town, Lewey Lake, Indian Lake, North Creek Ski Center, Fort William Henry, and many other Adirondack Mountain attractions.

NEW YORK

SECRET CAVERNS,
Box 88, Cobleskill.
Between U.S. Highway 20 and State
Highway 7, about
35 miles west of
Albany. Phone:
518-AF4-3431.

Courtesy of Secret Caverns, New York.

Secret Caverns is a fine example of a typical New York State cave. It has sinuous passageways with high domes, an active stream, and evidences of glacial action in the remains of gravel washed through the cave. Its natural entrance permits the visitor to see the division of the overlying limestone and the casts of fossils embedded in the stone. There is a waterfall in the cave which visitors see on the tour.

Open April 1 to November 1. During months of May, June, and September the hours are 9:00 A.M. to 7:00 P.M.; July and August, 8:00 A.M. to 9:00 P.M.; balance of season, 9:00 A.M. to 5:00 P.M.

Guided tour: 45 minutes.

Rates: adults, $1.25; children, $0.50. Group rates are available with notice.

On premises: snack bar, gift shop, camping, picnicking. *Nearby:* all facilities.

Nearby attractions: Old Stone Fort, Howe Caverns, Lower Adirondacks, Baseball Hall of Fame (Cooperstown), John Boyd Thacher State Park, New York State Museum, Schuyler Mansion, Cooperstown Indian Museum, James Fenimore Cooper Home.

Courtesy of Crystal Cave, Pennsylvania.

PENNSYLVANIA

CRYSTAL CAVE, 38 North 6th, Reading. Near Kutztown, midway between Reading and Allentown, U.S. 222 or U.S. 22. Phone: 215-683-3301.

Discovered in 1871 and commercialized since 1873, Crystal Cave is the oldest commercial cave in Pennsylvania. Situated on 125 acres of cave property, it is easily traversed along sloping concrete walks guarded by steel rails. Its accessibility to New York and Philadelphia makes it Pennsylvania's most popular cave. The cave formations in the foreground are known as "Prairie Dogs."

Open Febraury 15 to December 1 every day from 9:00 A.M. to 5:00 P.M., summer until 7:00 P.M.

Guided tour—30 to 45 minutes.

Rates: adults $2.00; children, $1.00. *Groups:* adults, $1.00; children, $0.50.

On premises: snack bar, gift shop, picnicking (100-table picnic park). *Nearby:* camping, motels, hotels.

Nearby attractions: W.K.&S. Steam Railroad, Roadside America, Blue Rocks, Onyx Cave, Hershey Park, Dorney's Park, Pagoda, Lehigh University, Muhlenberg College, Moravian College, Lafayette College, Kutztown State College, Albright College, Trexler Lehigh Game Preserve, Hawk Mountain.

Courtesy of Indian Caverns, Pennsylvania.

PENNSYLVANIA

INDIAN CAVERNS, Spruce Creek. On State Route 45 between State College and Water Street. Phone: 814-632-7578.

Indian Caverns, in beautiful Spruce Creek Valley, has nearly a mile of tourist passage. The cave has a long and authentic Indian history, as Spruce Creek Valley was a center of Shoshone Indian activity. An unusual number of Indian artifacts, some of which are shown here, have been found in the cave, and many of these are on display. The cave was commercialized in 1929.

Open all year from 9:00 A.M. to dusk.

Guided tour: one hour.

Rates: adults, $2.00; children, $1.00; groups of 25, 25% reduction.

On premises: soft drinks, gift shop, picnicking, fishing, hiking. *Nearby:* restaurant, camping, motels, hotels, cabins, trailer camp.

Nearby attractions: Lincoln Caverns, Pennsylvania State University, Bear Meadows State Forest, Alan Steeger State Forest, Greenwood Furnace State Park, Whipple Dam State Park, Horseshoe Curve, Swigart Auto Museum, Lanes Gun Museum, Christopher Columbus Chapel, Prince Gallitzia State Park, Trough Creek State Park, Detweiler Run State Forest, Penn's Cave, Woodward Cave, Black Moshannon State Park, East Broad Top Excursion R.R., Seldom Seen Coal Mine.

Courtesy of Indian Echo Caverns, Pennsylvania.

PENNSYLVANIA

INDIAN ECHO CAVERNS, P.O. Box 206, Hummelstown. U.S. 322-422 between Harrisburg and Hershey. Phone: 717-566-8131.

"Indian" in this cave's name refers to the Susquehannock Indians who lived in this area. The "Echo" is derived from the reverberations returning from the cave's walls. Seventeen hundred electric lights illuminate the cavern, which has many formations. It has been commercialized since 1929. The stalagmite in the center of the picture is said to be an Indian Chief addressing his warriors at a council meeting. *Open* daily May 1 to November 1; open weekends March, April, and November. Tour time is from 9:00 A.M. to dark.

Guided tour: 45 minutes.

Rates: adults, $1.55; children 6 to 12, $0.75. Group rates are available.

On premises: snack bar, gift shop, camping, picnicking. *Nearby:* restaurant, motels, hotel.

Nearby attractions: Harrisburg, Gettysburg, Indiantown Gap Military Reservation, Amish country, Hershey, Fort Hunter Museum, Carlisle Barracks, Molly Pitcher's Grave, Gifford Pinchot State Park, Lewis State Park, Susquehanna River, Lebanon Valley College, Ephrata Cloister, Weiser Park, Pennsylvania Farm Museum, Dickinson College, Pine Grove Furnace State Park, Hershey Museum, Hershey Park, Franklin and Marshall College, Strasburg Railroad.

Courtesy of Laurel Caverns, Pennsylvania.

PENNSYLVANIA

LAUREL CAVERNS, P.O. Box 1095, Uniontown. Off U.S. 40 east of Uniontown, 5 miles south of Summit Hotel. Phone: 412-329-5968.

For many years Dulany's Cave was a spelunker's paradise as hundreds of cave crawlers wandered through its corridors. With over 12 miles of passageway, it was not until 1964 that Dulany's was opened to the public under the name of Laurel Caverns. It has large rooms and serpentine passageways, and the tour wanders through chasms and canyons displayed to maximum advantage through the use of colored lights. The cave was discovered in the 1700's.

Open April 1 through November 16, 10:00 A.M. to 8:00 P.M. daily.
Guided tour: 30 minutes.
Rates: adults, $2.00; children, $1.00; group rates are available.
On premises: snack bar, gift shop, camping, picnicking, trailer camp. *Nearby:* hotel, motels.
Nearby attractions: Fort Necessity, Fallingwaters Estate, Ohiopyle State Park, Albert Galatin Home, Braddock's Grave, Mount Davis State Forest, Laurel Hill State Park, Kooser State Park, West Virginia University (West Verginia), Mount Chateau State Park (West Virginia), Youghiougheny Reservoir, steel mills.

PENNSYLVANIA

LINCOLN CAVERNS,

directly on U.S. 22,
about 3 miles west
of Huntington.
Phone:
814-643-0268.

Courtesy of Lincoln Caverns, Pennsylvania.

Lincoln Caverns was discovered in 1930 by roadbuilders, and the entrance is just 40 feet off the highway. Frequent new discoveries in the cave have been made since that date, and a 1941 discovery was opened to the public in 1963, adding a new section to the tour. The cave is on two levels. Some sections have ultraviolet lights to obtain unusual effects. Shown in the photograph is the "Bath of Nymphs."

Open all year except January and February, when the cave can be seen by appointment only. Open from 9:00 A.M. to 7:00 P.M. from May until September and from 9:00 A.M. to 5:00 P.M. at other times.

Guided tour: 50 minutes.

Rates: adults $2.00; children, $1.00; group rates are available.

On premises: snack bar, gift shop, picnicking. *Nearby:* restaurant, camping, motels, hotels, cabins, trailer camp.

Nearby attractions: Indian Caverns, Pennsylvania State University, Bear Meadows State Forest, Alan Steeger State Forest, Greenwood Furnace State Park, Whipple Dam State Park, Horseshoe Curve, Swigart Auto Museum, Lanes Gun Museum, Christopher Columbus Chapel, Prince Gallitzia State Park, Trough Creek State Park, Detweiler Run State Forest, Penn's Cave, Woodward Cave, Black Moshannon State Park, East Broad Top Excursion R.R.

Courtesy of Lost River Caverns, Pennsylvania.

PENNSYLVANIA

LOST RIVER CAVERNS, Hellertown. Off State Route 412, about 3 miles from Bethlehem. Phone: 215-838-8767.

The cavern received its name from a lost river—an underground stream that flows along the length of the cave. In one room in the cave is a fluorescent mineral display. At the entrance lobby are hanging tropical gardens housed under a glass roof. A mass of solid rock flowstone looks like a glacier creeping its way down the side of a mountain.

Open all year, 9:00 A.M. to 9:00 P.M.

Guided tour: 30 to 45 minutes.

Rates: adults, $1.65; children, $0.75. Special rates for groups.

On premises: Gilman Museum (free), rock and mineral store, lapidary shop, snack bar, gift shop, camping, trailer camp (two-day limit free), picnicking. *Nearby:* restaurant, motel, hotel, cabins, swimming pool.

Nearby attractions: Crystal Cave, Onyx Cave, Valley Forge, Hopewell Village National Historic Site, Ralph Stover State Park, Washington Crossing, Roosevelt State Park, Delaware Water Gap, Lafayette College, Lehigh University, Voorhees State Park (New Jersey).

PENNSYLVANIA

ONYX CAVE,
RD 2, Box 308,
Hamburg. Off State
Route 662, about 3
miles south of U.S. 22
in Hamburg. Phone:
215-562-4335.

Courtesy of Onyx Cave, Pennsylvania.

Onyx Cave was discovered in 1873, after the Civil War, by workmen blasting in a limestone quarry. The cave is almost 1,000 feet long, with many side passages. The resemblance to an elephant's head can easily be seen at the left center of the photograph in the "Elephant's Head Room."
Open May 1 through October 30 from 9:00 A.M. to 7:00 P.M.
Guided tour: 30 minutes,
Rates: adults, $1.30; children, $0.65. Groups of 15 or more: adults, $1.00; children, $0.65.
On premises: snack bar, gift shop, picnicking. *Nearby:* restaurant, camping, motels, hotels, cabins, trailer camp.
Nearby attractions: Crystal Cave, Blue Rocks, Roadside America, Lost River Cave, Valley Forge, Hopewell Village National Historical Site, French Creek State Park, W.K.&S. Steam Railway, Hershey Park, Doney's Park, Pagoda, Hawk Mountain Sanctuary, Hawk Mountain Railroad Line.

Courtesy of Penn's Cave, Pennsylvania.

PENNSYLVANIA

PENN'S CAVE, Centre Hall. 5 miles east of Centre Hall on State Route 192. Phone: 814-364-1664.

Penn's Cave is unusual in that the entire one-mile trip is made by motorboat. At the entrance is an immense spring of unknown origin that flows into and through the cave. The cave has been commercialized since 1885. In the center of the photograph you will see "The Statue of Liberty."

Open all year from 9:00 A.M. to 5:00 P.M. except from Memorial Day to Labor Day, when it is open until 8:00 P.M.

Guided boat trip: 45 minutes.

Rates: adults, $2.00; children, $1.00; groups of 25 or more, $1.50 each.

On premises: restaurant, snack bar, gift shop, camping, picnicking. *Nearby:* motels, hotel, cabins, trailer camp.

Nearby attractions: Poe Paddy State Park, Penn's View, Skimont, Winter's State Park, Joyce Kilmer's birthplace, Detweiler Run State Forest, Pennsylvania State University, Fisherman's Paradise, Woodward Cave, Nittany Mountain, Black Moshannon State Park, Big Spring, Boal Museum, fish hatcheries.

PENNSYLVANIA

WONDERLAND CAVERNS,

Manns Choice.
A short distance east of State Route 31 at Manns Choice, 7 miles west of Bedford. Phone: 814-823-6882

Courtesy of Wonderland Caverns, Pennsylvania.

Commercialized since 1932, Wonderland Caverns is one of the few coral-reef caves open to the public. The cave contains many fossils and formations, and features a dinosaur-like imprint 100 feet long and 25 feet high.

Open from May 30 to October 15, 9:00 A.M. to 6:00 P.M.

Guided tour: 35 minutes.

Rates: adults, $1.50; children, $0.75; groups of 20 or more, $0.75 each.

On premises: picnicking. *Nearby:* restaurant, motel, cabins, trailer camp.

Nearby attractions: Martin Hill State Forest, Quomahoning Reservoir, Blue Knob State Park, Fort Tonoloway State Park (Maryland), Shawnee State Park, Bedford Resort Area.

Courtesy of Woodward Cave, Pennsylvania.

PENNSYLVANIA

WOODWARD CAVE, Woodward. 1½ miles off Route 45 at Woodward, 25 miles west of Lewisburg. Phone: 814-349-5185.

In the past, Woodward Cave would flood when Pine Creek overflowed. Now a new channel has been constructed, directing the stream away from the cave. The tour covers about ½ mile, with some interesting formations to be seen. Concentric rings formed by the slowly dripping water in Crystal Lake can clearly be seen in the photograph.

Open April 15 to November 1, 9:00 A.M. to 9:00 P.M. daily.

Guided tour: 45 minutes.

Rates: adults, $1.55; children, $0.75; group rates available.

On premises: snack bar, gift shop, camping, cabins, trailer camp, picnicking, sports area. *Nearby:* restaurant, motels, hotel.

Nearby attractions: Poe Valley State Park, Penn's View, Nittany Mountain, Black Moshannon State Park, Big Spring, Penn's Cave, Boal Museum, Skimont, Winter's State Park, Joyce Kilmer's birthplace, Detweiler Run State Forest, Pennsylvania State University, Bucknell University, Fisherman's Paradise, Prince Gallitzia State Park, Trough Creek State Park, fish hatcheries.

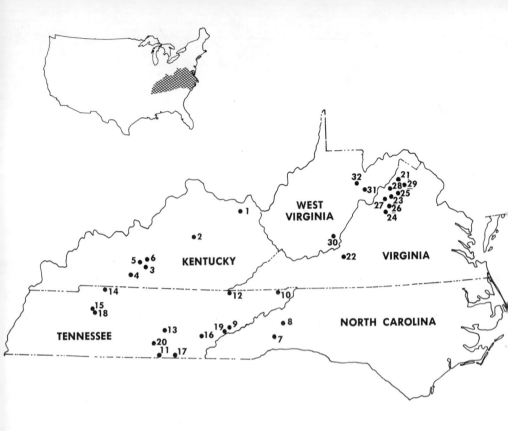

1. Carter Caves, Kentucky
2. Daniel Boone's Cave, Kentucky
3. Diamond Caverns, Kentucky
4. Lost River Cave, Kentucky
5. Mammoth Cave National Park, Kentucky
6. Mammoth Onyx Cave, Kentucky
7. Chimney Rock Park, North Carolina
8. Linville Caverns, North Carolina
9. Alum Cave, Tennessee
10. Bristol Caverns, Tennessee
11. Crystal Cave, Tennessee
12. Cudjo's Cave, Tennessee
13. Cumberland Caverns, Tennessee
14. Dunbar Cave, Tennessee
15. Jewel Cave, Tennessee
16. The Lost Sea, Tennessee
17. Ruby Falls, Tennessee
18. Ruskin Cave, Tennessee
19. Tuckaleechee Caverns, Tennessee
20. Wonder Cave, Tennessee
21. Battlefield Crystal Caverns, Virginia
22. Dixie Caverns, Virginia
23. Endless Caverns, Virginia
24. Grand Caverns, Virginia
25. Luray Caverns, Virginia
26. Massanutten Caverns, Virginia
27. Melrose Caverns, Virginia
28. Shenandoah Caverns, Virginia
29. Skyline Caverns, Virginia
30. Organ Cave, West Virginia
31. Seneca Caverns, West Virginia
32. Smoke Hole Cavern, West Virginia

2. MID-ATLANTIC REGION

Kentucky
North Carolina
Tennessee
Virginia
West Virginia

Some of the finest caves in the United States are found in this region, which had a favorable climate for their formation. The humid midlands, forest cover, limestone matrix, and freedom from the effects of long freezing during the advance and retreat of the glaciers richly endowed this section of the country. In Virginia and West Virginia these favorable conditions produced the highly decorated, scenic, and very beautiful caves clustered along the slopes of the limestone valleys. In Kentucky, in the Mammoth Cave region, a 50-foot sandstone cap over the entire limestone region formed a protecting cover that permitted development of cave systems unequaled in the world in size. Miles and miles of tunnels in distinct levels show the effects of erosion and of solution by underground water, and provide scientists with a glimpse of how the growth of major cave systems evolved. Because the sandstone cap often prevented the development of decorations except where the cover was cracked, miles of these tunnels are apt to be completely bare and without formations.

KENTUCKY

CARTER CAVES, Carter Caves State Park, Olive Hill. 4 miles from U.S. 60 on Kentucky 182. The intersection of these two highways is 6 miles from Olive Hill and 10 miles from Grayson. **CASCADE CAVES** is on Highway 209 off U.S. 60. Phone: 606-286-4411.

This beautiful state-owned park contains a number of caves open to the public, three of which are lighted, and serviced by guides. Cascade Caves is now part of the state park. Formerly it was operated privately as a commercial cave. X Cave has been lighted, as well as Saltpeter Cave. In addition to the lighted caves, there are several other caves open to qualified visitors. Entry to these caves requires special permission and the use of the visitors' own lights. Notable among these are Bat Cave and Laurel Cave.

Open April 15 to October 31 from 8:00 A.M. to 6:30 P.M. Cascade Caves: open from June 1 to Labor Day.

Guided tours as noted in each cave: 30 minutes to 1 hour.

Rates: (each cave) adults, $0.75; children under 12, $0.35.

Combination tour (three caves): adults, $1.50; children, $0.75.

On premises: restaurant, snack bar, gift shop, camping, lodge, cabins, trailer camp, picnicking, baby sitters, full-time naturalist (June 1–September 15). *Nearby:* scattered facilities.

Nearby attractions: Greenbo Lake State Park, Roosevelt Shawnee State Park (Ohio), Ashland, Portsmouth (Ohio), Roosevelt State Reservoir (Ohio).

Courtesy of Daniel Boone's Cave, Kentucky.

KENTUCKY

DANIEL BOONE'S CAVE, Nicholasville. On U.S. 27, about 20 miles south of Lexington, 7 miles south of Nicholasville. Phone: 606-885-4764.

Daniel Boone's Cave is about ½ mile long, with openings at each end. What is known as the entrance is on a cliffside. In 1776 Daniel Boone, being chased by Indians, lowered himself to the cliffside entrance and escaped from the rear exit of the cave, which was unknown to the Indians. At one time Boone had a fort nearby, but this has since been destroyed. The group of stalagmites in the foreground is known as the "Old Hen and Little Chickens."

Open April through September, 9:00 A.M. to 7:00 P.M.

Guided tour: 35 minutes.

Rates: adults, $0.90; children; $0.60; groups, $0.60.

On premises: gift shop, picnicking. *Nearby:* restaurant, motels, hotels.

Nearby attractions: Blue Grass Country, 300 horse farms; Camp Nelson National Cemetery, Daniel Boone's Grave, Georgetown College, Fort Brannaum, Kentucky Palisades, Herrington Lake, University of Kentucky, Transylvania College, East Kentucky State College, Bird and Animal Forest, Perryville Battlefield, racehorse country.

KENTUCKY

DIAMOND CAVERNS, Park City. On State Highway 255, about 1½ miles from Park City. Phone: 502-749-2891.

Diamond Caverns recently extended the length of the trip owing to new discoveries. The cave is well decorated. The owners also operate Jan Cave, into which lodge guests are driven nightly on a Nature Ride. Diamond Caverns is entered through the lobby of Colonial Lodge.

Open all year.

Guided tour: 1½ hours.

Rates: adults, $2.00; children 9 to 14, $1.00; under 9, free.

On premises: restaurant, gift shop, motel (lodge), hotel, picnicking, swimming pool.

Nearby: all facilities in Park City.

Nearby attractions: Mammoth Cave National Park, scenic boat trips in Mammoth Cave National Park on Green River, Mammoth Onyx Cave, Lost River Cave, Abraham Lincoln National Historical Site, resort area.

KENTUCKY

LOST RIVER CAVE,
RFD 4, Bowling
Green. U.S. 31W
south of Bowling
Green. Phone:
502-842-3809.

Courtesy of Lost River Cave, Kentucky.

Lost River Cave was one of Jesse James's many hideouts. In 1868 he hid in this cave after robbing the bank in Russellville. The cave has a river and a spring.
Open 11 months from 8:00 A.M. to 9:00 P.M.
Guided tour: 30 minutes.
Rates: adults, $0.50; children, $0.25.
On premises: gift shop. *Nearby:* all facilities in Bowling Green.
Nearby attractions: Mammoth Onyx Cave, Lake Malone State Park, Western Kentucky State College, Barren River Lake, Shaker Museum, Beach Bend Zoo, Mammoth Cave National Park, Diamond Caverns, amusement center.

47

KENTUCKY

MAMMOTH CAVE NATIONAL PARK, Mammoth Cave. From Park City take State Highway 255 to park entrance. From there it is 5 miles to park headquarters. From Cave City take State Highway 70 ten miles to park headquarters. Phone: 502-758-2251.

While large portions of Mammoth Cave are unadorned, it is nevertheless one of the world's most interesting caverns. Its reputed 150 miles of passageway are, of course, not all open to the public, but the many trips scheduled for visitors offer a variety not found in any cave in the world. For those interested in the scenic values of the cave the Frozen Niagara trip is recommended. This is the easiest and shortest trip, and it includes an impressive assortment of formations, especially the 75-foot-high Frozen Niagara, the largest known travertine formation in the cave.

The Historic Trip features: the saltpeter vats of the War of 1812; the world's first tubercular hospital, which was established in the cave in the mistaken belief that the pure air would be a cure-all; and Indian culture and artifacts found in the cave, including a 2,000-year-old mummy.

The Echo River Trip winds into the cave, 360 feet below the surface, and includes a boat ride at this level on Echo River. Here visitors will see the famous blindfish of Mammoth Cave.

Those wishing a longer and more strenuous scenic trip will enjoy the Scenic Trip, which includes the features of the Frozen Niagara trip plus many others, and lunch in the Snowball Room where food is brought from the surface by a 267-foot elevator.

The All-Day Trip includes the features of all of the other trips.

In all there are six trips described. Note the child and family rates below.

Frozen Niagara Trip: distance, ¾ mile; time required, 1½ hours. Descent of 250 feet by stairway; trip features pits, domes, "Frozen Niagara," Crystal Lake. Summer, 9 trips daily; winter, 5 trips daily. First trip, 8:00 A.M.; last trip, 4:00 P.M. *Rate:* $1.85.

Historic Trip: distance, 1½ miles; time required, about 1½ hours. Considered the easiest trip, with 65 steps. Includes saltpeter mining vats of War of 1812, Indian "mummy," other historic points. Summer, 2 trips daily at 11:30 A.M. and 3:00 P.M.; winter, 1 trip daily at 12:00 noon. *Rate:* $1.50.

Echo River Trip (pictured): distance, 3 miles; time required, 3 hours. Some strenuous climbing. Trip includes "Historic Entrance," "Rotunda," "Bottomless Pit," "Fat Man's Misery," "Mammoth Dome," and boat ride on Echo River. Summer trips only; four trips daily. First trip, 9:00 A.M.; last trip, 3:00 P.M. Rate: $1.50.

Mammoth Dome Trip: distance, 2¼ miles; time required, 2 hours. Some strenuous climbing. Trip includes "Rotunda," "Bottomless Pit," "Fat Man's Misery," etc. Winter trips only; four trips daily. First trip, 9:00 A.M.; last trip, 3:00 P.M. *Rate:* $1.50.

Scenic Trip: distance, 4½ miles; time required, about 4½ hours. A strenuous trip featuring "Cleveland Avenue," "Diamond Grotto," "Boone Avenue," "Frozen Niagara," as well as deposits of gypsum and other cave formations. Lunch available in Snowball Dining Room 267 feet underground. Summer, 2 trips daily at 8:30 A.M. and 1:45 P.M.; winter, 1 trip at 11:00 A.M. *Rate:* $2.35.

All Day Trip: distance, 7 miles; time required, 6½ hours. A strenuous trip. Most of the features of the Echo River and "Frozen Niagara" trips are included. Lunch in Snowball Dining Room. Summer only: 2 trips daily at 8:00 A.M. and 10:00 A.M. *Rate:* $2.85.

Summer schedule May 30 to Labor Day; winter schedule Labor Day through May 29.

Adults are all persons over 16. Children under 16 accompanied by adult, no charge. Family group rates are available. School groups admitted free upon advance application.

On premises: restaurant, snack bar, gift shop, photo shop, camping, motel, hotel, underground restaurant, trailer camp, cabins, lodge, cottages, picnicking, nature trails. *Nearby:* all facilities.

Nearby attractions: Scenic boat trips in the park on Green River, Mammoth Onyx Cave, Diamond Caverns, Lost River Cave, Abraham Lincoln National Historical Site, resort area.

Courtesy of National Park Concessions, Inc. Photo by W. Ray Scott.

KENTUCKY

MAMMOTH ONYX CAVE,

Box 527, Horse Cave. At Horse Cave Interchange, Interstate 65 and State 335, about 3 miles west of Horse Cave. Phone: 502-786-2634.

Courtesy of Mammoth Onyx Cave, Kentucky.

Mammoth Onyx Cave was discovered in 1799 and commercialized in 1921. It is particularly suitable for easy viewing, being quite level and requiring only fourteen steps to enter. A stream of clear green water runs through the cave, and sharp-eyed visitors may catch glimpses of blind fish, salamanders, or white crayfish. It has many small rimstone pools. The cave is in a 300-acre Wildlife Reservation a short distance from Mammoth Cave National Park. There is a small wildlife display on the property. Pictured here is "Martha's Pool" in "Founders Hall."

Open all year every day from 8:00 A.M. to 5:00 P.M.

Guided tour: 1 hour.

Rates: adults, $2.06; children, $1.03; groups of 10 or more, $1.03 by prior arrangement.

On premises: gift shop, picnicking, wildlife display, overnight camping and trailer camp for cave visitors only. *Nearby:* motels, hotels, baby sitters, restaurant.

Nearby attractions: Abraham Lincoln Birthplace National Historic Site, Western Kentucky University, Mammoth Cave National Park, Diamond Caverns, Nolin Reservoir, Barren River Lake State Park.

Courtesy of Chimney Rock Park, North Carolina.

NORTH CAROLINA

CHIMNEY ROCK PARK, Chimney Rock. Off U.S. 74-64 and State 9 about 22 miles southeast of Asheville.

Chimney Rock Park is a scenic area of massive rocks, waterfalls, nature trails, and panoramic views. A tunnel blasted 196 feet through solid granite leads to an elevator to take visitors to the top. A minor part of the area is Moonshiner's Cave near the base of Chimney Rock. The stairway leads down to where there was once a still.

Open March 15 to December 15; in summer from 7:30 A.M. to 5:30 P.M., in winter from 8:00 A.M. to 4:30 P.M.

Self-guided tour: no lights required.

Rates: adults, $0.90; children, $0.45; groups of 20 or more, $0.75. (Rates are for entire Chimney Rock Park, including cave.)

On premises: food-vending machines, gift shop, picnicking, nature trails, jeep rides.

Nearby: camping, motels, hotels, cabins, trailer camp.

Nearby attractions: Museum of North Carolina Minerals, Mount Mitchell (highest point east of the Mississippi) State Park, Cowpens National Battlefield Site (South Carolina), Pleasant Ridge State Park (South Carolina), Lake Lure, Biltmore House and Gardens (Asheville), Linville Caverns (forty-five miles).

NORTH CAROLINA

LINVILLE CAVERNS, Ashford. On U.S. 221, about 18 miles north of Marion.

Linville Caverns was discovered 100 years ago when the mysterious appearance of fish swimming out of a mountainside stream led explorers deep into the mountain. During the Civil War the caverns served as a hiding place for deserters from both armies, and an old man made and mended shoes in the cave for the soldiers. *Open* all year from 7:00 A.M. to dusk.
Guided tour: 45 minutes to an hour.
Rates: adults, $1.00; children, $0.50; group rates, 25 or more, $0.75.
On premises: gift shop, picnicking. *Nearby:* restaurant, snack bar, camping, motels, hotel, cabins, trailer camp.
Nearby attractions: Grandfather Mountain, Blowing Rock, Tweetsie Railroad, Horn in the West, Little Switzerland, Lake Tahoma, Linville Falls, Lake James, Grassy Gardens, Chimney Rock Park, Mount Mitchell (highest point in North Carolina), Mount Mitchell (highest point east of the Mississippi) State Park, Museum of North Carolina Minerals, Rice Creek State Park (Tennessee), Dennis Cave State Park (Tennessee), Moses H. Cone Park, Blue Ridge Parkway.

TENNESSEE

ALUM CAVE, Great Smoky National Park, Gatlinburg. On U.S. 441 in Smoky National Park

Many tourists inquire about Alum Cave. This is not a true cave, but a large overhanging bluff along what is known as Alum Cave Trail. Information can be obtained from Park Headquarters or any Park Ranger. The trail is one for self-guidance, has markers, and is about 5½ miles long.

Courtesy of Bristol Caverns, Tennessee.

TENNESSEE

BRISTOL CAVERNS, Route No. 3, Bristol. On U.S. 421 about 5 miles southeast of Bristol. Phone: 615-764-1646.

Bristol Caverns was used by Indians as an attack and escape route in the frontier days. In those days the cave was known as Underground River, and the present tour follows portions of the river, crossing it at points via bridges from which reflections in the quiet river waters can be seen. The Guardsmen of the Trail are aligned along the tourist path in the photograph.

Open all year from 9:30 A.M. to 6:00 P.M. except Sundays from 12 noon to 6:00 P.M. *Guided tour:* 1 hour.

Rates: adults, $1.50; children, 7 through 12, $0.90; under 7, free. Groups of 20, $0.50 each.

On premises: snack bar, gift shop, picnicking. *Nearby:* restaurant, camping, motels, hotels, cabins, trailer camp, baby sitters.

Nearby attractions: South Holston Lake, Rocky Mount, Boone Lake, Watauge Lake, Barter Theater, Patrick Henry Lake, Warrior's Path State Park, Natural Tunnel (Virginia), Emory and Henry College (Virginia).

TENNESSEE

CRYSTAL CAVE, Route 4, Cummings Highway, Chattanooga. On U.S. 41-64 and 72, about 4½ miles west of Chattanooga. Phone: 615-821-2570.

The entrance to Crystal Cave is housed in a large base station building from which the cave owners also operate the Chattanooga Skyride, popularly known as the Mount Aetna Skyride. It ascends 2,800 feet from the cave entrance to the summit of Mount Aetna. The large cave is developed along five levels. Visitors are greeted by Creek Indians, who give Indian dance performances. The rates given are for cave tours only, and do not include the Skyride, for which there is an additional charge of $1.50. A cave guide is perched high above the tourist path in this portion of the "Rock Mountain Winter Scene" room of the cave.

Open all year from 8:00 A.M. to 9:00 P.M.

Guided tour: 30 minutes.

Rates: adults, $1.50; children, $0.75; groups of 15 or more, $0.75.

On premises: restaurant, gift shop, camping, picnicking, Indian dances, skyride.

Nearby: all facilities in and near Chattanooga. Reservations in season advisable.

Nearby attractions: Rock City and Gardens, Lookout Mountain Incline Railway, Confederama, Chattanooga-Chickamauga National Cemetery (Georgia), Chickamauga Lake and Dam, Russell Cave National Monument (Alabama), Cathedral Caverns (Alabama), Crystal Cave, Wonder Cave, Harrison Bay State Park, Booker T. Washington State Park, Lookout Mountain, Signal Mountain, University of Chattanooga, Southern Missionary College, Tennessee Temple College, Lake Winnepesaukah, Hales Bar Dam and Lake, Nickajack Lake and Dam, Cloudland Canyon State Park (Georgia).

CUDJO'S CAVE, Cumberland Gap. On U.S. 25 east
in Cumberland Gap. Phone: 703-761-2203.

Situated almost exactly on the tricorner of Tennessee, Virginia, and Kentucky, Cudjo's Cave overlooks Cumberland Gap National Historical Park, scene of many Civil War battles. It is halfway up Pinnacle Mountain, the gateway to Cumberland Gap. Early settlers used to hold dances in the "Ballroom" in the cave.

Open all year, 8:00 A.M. to 5:00 P.M.

Guided tour: 45 minutes.

Rates: adults, $1.00; children 6 through 12, $0.50.

On premises: gift shop. *Nearby:* all facilities in Cumberland Gap.

Nearby attractions: Fern Lake, Pine Mountain State Park (Kentucky), Big Ridge State Park, Lincoln Memorial University, Norris Lake, Norris Dam, Cherokee Lake, Natural Tunnel (Virginia), coalfields.

TENNESSEE

CUMBERLAND CAVERNS,
McMinnville. 8 miles east of McMinnville just off State Highway 8. Phone: 615-668-4396.

*Courtesy of
Cumberland Caverns,
Tennessee.*

Known since 1810 as Higgenbotham Cave, the cavern had been a spelunkers' paradise until 1956 when it was opened for tourists. Although Cumberland Caverns is actually a vast cave system—with 16 miles of explored passageways—the most interesting portions are covered on the commercial tour. Mined extensively for saltpeter during the Civil War, the workings still remain, and visitors may see the leaching vats, tools and wooden pipes used by the miners. An "Underground Dining Room," complete with all furnishings, including candlelighted tables, has been set up in a cave room, which is 600 feet long and 150 feet wide. This room, the "Hall of the Mountain King," has a 140-foot-high ceiling. The cave has been the source of much eyeless cave life, blind fish, salamanders, and arthropoda. Part of the "Cathedral Room," profusely decorated with giant stalactites, stalagmites, columns, and draperies, is seen in the photograph.

Open daily April 1 to October 31, weekends only, November 1 to March 31, 8:00 A.M. to 5:00 P.M.

Guided tour: 1½ hours.

Rates: adults, $1.75; children, $1.00; groups (25 or more), adults, $1.25; children, $0.75. Special rates for Scouts. Overnight camping in cave is permitted by arrangement for Scouts, schools, and groups.

On premises: snack bar, gift shop, camping, picnicking. *Nearby:* restaurant, motels, hotels, cabins, trailer camp.

Nearby attractions: Fall Creek State Park, Center Hill Reservoir, Rock Island Lakes, Cumberland Mountain State Park, Wonder Cave, resort areas.

DUNBAR CAVE, Route 3, Clarksville. Off Highway 79, about 4 miles east of Clarksville. Phone: 615-647-3663 or 647-3612.

Discovered in 1790, Dunbar Cave has a history of Indian lore and saltpeter mining. The cave has been a hideout for the Confederate Army during the Civil War, a counterfeiters' base, and a dance pavilion. In 1851, Jenny Lind sang at the cave and left her signature upon its walls. In 1943, development of the cave area as a resort was begun, at which time it was acquired by Roy Acuff of Grand Ole Opry fame. It is known to have 7½ miles of passage, and features an underground river.

Open May to September from 10:00 A.M. to 6:00 P.M. daily.

Guided tour: 45 minutes to an hour.

Rates: adults, $1.00; children, $0.50. Group rates available.

On premises: snack bar, gift shop, swimming pool, 15-acre lake for boating and fishing. *Nearby:* all other facilities.

Nearby attractions: Ruskin Cave, Jewel Cave, Tennessee River, Fort Campbell Military Reservation, Montgomery Bell State Park, Jefferson Davis Monument.

Courtesy of Jewel Cave, Tennessee.

TENNESSEE

JEWEL CAVE, RFD 3, Box 180, Dickson. About 12 miles northwest of Dickson between U.S. 70 and State Highway 49 on Yellow Creek Road. No phone.

Many fossils have been found in and near Jewel Cave. On display are prehistoric cave-bear bones. In this well-decorated cave, prehistoric bear, wolf, and peccary bones can be seen under six inches of flowstone. The tourist path directly traverses the profusely decorated "Palace of the Gods."

Open all year during daylight.

Guided tour: 1 hour. Other trips in groups of five by appointment.

Rates: adults, $1.00; children under 12, $0.50. Group rates available.

On premises: snack bar, gift shop, picnicking. *Nearby:* all facilities, swimming, dancing.

Nearby attractions: Dunbar Cave, Jefferson Davis Monument, Donelson National Military Park and Cemetery, Fort Campbell Military Reservation, Montgomery Bell State Park, Ruskin Cave.

Courtesy of The Lost Sea, Tennessee.

TENNESSEE

THE LOST SEA, P.O. Box 106, Sweetwater. On Craighead Highway, 5 miles from either Sweetwater, on U.S. 11, or Madisonville, on U.S. 411. Phone: 615-337-7126.

Previously known as Craighead Caverns, this cave was reopened in 1965 as The Lost Sea. The "sea" is a 4½-acre lake 1,000 feet from the entrance, and contains over 30,000,000 gallons of water. It is believed to be the world's largest underground lake. By means of underwater lighting, huge rainbow trout, said to be the largest in the eastern United States, can be seen through glass-bottom boats, which are used on the cave tour. The boats shown here are powered by silent electric motors operating at slow speed to give visitors ample time to examine the depths of the lake and the fish. Boats accommodate thirty people, and operate continuously. Preceding the boat ride, visitors are guided past an old saltpeter mine, a bootlegger's still, and other relics in the cave. On display in the cave, on the spot on which the original was found, is a replica of a Pleistocene jaguar. Its complete skeleton was removed and taken to the American Museum of Natural History in New York.

Open all year: summer, 8:00 A.M. to 7:00 P.M.; winter, 9:00 A.M. to 5:00 P.M.
Guided tour: 1¼ hours, including boat ride.
Rates: adults, $2.25; children, $1.25. Group rates available.
On premises: snack bar, gift shop, camping, picnicking. *Nearby:* restaurants, motels, hotel.
Nearby attractions: Oxone Falls, American Museum of Atomic Energy (Oak Ridge), Tuckaleechee Caverns, Great Smoky National Park, Watts Bar Lake and Dam, Fort Loudoun, Cherokee National Forest, Tellico Plains Resort, Cherokee National Forest, Tennessee Village of the 1800's, Tennessee River, Quinn Springs State Park, University of Tennessee, Chilhowee State Park, Knoxville College.

TENNESSEE

RUBY FALLS (LOOKOUT MOUNTAIN CAVERNS),
Route 4,
Chattanooga. State
Route 148 just off
U.S. 11, 41, 64, 72,
and near Interstates
25, 59, and 75.
Phone:
615-821-6731.

*Courtesy of
Ruby Falls
(Lookout Mountain
Caverns), Tennessee.*

The natural entrance of these twin caves was sealed by the construction of a railroad tunnel through Lookout Mountain. In 1923, an elevator shaft was drilled through the solid rock to make the caves accessible to the public. It was at this time that the famous Ruby Falls, pictured here, was discovered 1,120 feet below the surface, and dropping a sheer 145 feet, creating a spectacular underground scene. Since the original entrance was off the banks of the Tennessee River, the caves were easily entered by Indians and Civil War soldiers, many of whom wrote on the walls. Many other people have left their names inscribed on the sides of the cave; the most prominent signature is that of Andrew Jackson, dated 1833. A safe and modern elevator takes visitors to the Ruby Falls level and makes sight-seeing easy for children and elderly people.

Open all year, 7:00 A.M. to 11:00 P.M. in summer, and 8:00 A.M. to 9:00 P.M. in winter.

Guided tour: 40 to 45 minutes.

Rates: adults, $1.50; children 6 through 12, $0.75; children under 6, free. Groups: Student groups of 15 or more, $0.75; other groups of 15 or more, $1.00.

On premises: snack bar, gift shop. *Nearby:* restaurants, motels, picnicking.

Nearby attractions: Rock City Gardens, Lookout Mountain Incline Railway, Confederama, Chattanooga-Chickamauga National Military Park (Georgia), Chickamauga Lake and Dam, Russell Cave National Monument (Alabama), Cathedral Caverns (Alabama), Crystal Cave, Wonder Cave, Harrison Bay State Park, Booker T. Washington State Park, Lookout Mountain, Signal Mountain, University of Chattanooga, Southern Missionary College, Tennessee Temple College, Lake Winnepesaukah, Hales Bar Dam and Lake, Nickajack Lake and Dam, Cloudland Canyon State Park (Georgia).

Courtesy of Ruskin Cave, Tennessee.

TENNESSEE

RUSKIN CAVE, Route 3, Dickson. About 6 miles northwest of Dickson between U.S. 70 and State Route 49 on Yellow Creek Road. Phone: 615-242-1777.

Ruskin Cave is part of the Ruskin resort and vacation area. The cave contains a large entrance room that can seat 1,000 people. Square dances are held every Saturday night in the cave entrance. The cave is undeveloped.

Open all year from 9:00 A.M. to dark.

Self-guided tours, except in entrance room. Bring your own lights for further exploration.

Rates: adults, $1.00; children, $0.50; groups, $0.50 each.

On premises: restaurant, snack bar, gift shop, camping, cabins, trailer camp, picnicking, swimming pool, recreational area. *Nearby:* motels, hotel.

Nearby attractions: Dunbar Cave, Jewel Cave, Jefferson Davis Monument, Donelson National Military Park and Cemetery, Fort Campbell Military Reservation, Montgomery Bell State Park, Kentucky Lake, fishing, swimming.

TENNESSEE

TUCKALEECHEE CAVERNS,
Route 1, Townsend.
Off State Highway
73 near Great
Smoky Mountains
National Park.
Phone:
615-448-2274.

Courtesy of Tuckaleechee Caverns, Tennessee.

Tuckaleechee means "Peaceful Valley," and it was in this valley that the Cherokee Indians lived. Their descendants still live on the Qualla Reservation near Smoky Mountain National Park. Tuckaleechee Caverns contains a rushing river that is followed for part of the cave tour. The cave was opened to the public in 1953, and a year later the largest room in the cavern was discovered and opened for visitors. Flowstone Falls, shown in the photograph, is a masterpiece of nature, a curtain of beautiful flowing onyx.

Open daily from April 1 through October from 9:00 A.M. to 6:00 P.M.

Guided tour: 1 hour.

Rates: adults, $1.50; children, $0.50; groups of 15, $1.00 each for adults.

On premises: gift shop, camping, picnicking. *Nearby:* restaurants, snack bars, motels, hotels, cabins, trailer camps.

Nearby attractions: University of Tennessee, American Museum of Atomic Energy (Oak Ridge), Fort Loudoun Lake, Douglas Lake, Knoxville College, Smoky Sky Lift, Christmas Gardens, Maryville College, Sam Houston Schoolhouse, Goldrush Junction, Fabulous Fairyland, Pigeon Forge Pottery, Old Mill, Great Smoky National Park, Gatlinburg Resort Area, The Lost Sea, Joyce Kilmer Memorial Forest (North Carolina), Fontana Lake and Dam.

TENNESSEE

WONDER CAVE, Monteagle. On U.S. 41, about 4
miles north of Monteagle. Phone: 615-467-3530.

Commercialized since 1900, three years after its discovery, Wonder Cave is one
of the first commercialized caves in the Sòuth. It has an underground river.
Open all year, 7:00 A.M. to dusk.
Guided tour: 1 hour.
Rates: adults, $2.00; children, $0.85. Groups: adults, $1.00; children, $0.50.
On premises: gift shop, camping, trailer camp, picnicking, antique shop. *Nearby:*
restaurant, snack bar, motels, hotels, cabins.
Nearby attractions: Arnold Space Center, University of the South, Cumberland
Caverns, Russell Cave (Alabama), Sequoyah Cave (Alabama), Ruby Falls–Lookout Mountain Cave, Crystal Cave, Rock City and Gardens, Lookout Mountain
Incline Railway, Confederama, Lookout Mountain, University of Chattanooga, Signal
Mountain.

VIRGINIA

BATTLEFIELD CRYSTAL CAVERNS, Strasburg. On
U.S. Route 11. Phone: 703-465-3633.

Once known as Hupp's Cave, Battlefield Crystal Caverns lies beneath the site
of a great Civil War battle known as the Battle of Cedar Creek. The breastworks
and artillery pits of the conflict can be seen on the cavern grounds.
Open all year, from 8:00 A.M. to 6:00 P.M.
Guided tour: 30 minutes.
Rates: adults and children, $1.25 plus tax. No group rates.
On premises: snack bar, picnicking. *Nearby:* restaurants, motels, hotels, camping,
trailer camp.
Nearby attractions: Smoke Hole Caverns (West Virginia), Shenandoah Caverns,
Endless Caverns, Luray Caverns, Skyline Caverns, Site of John Brown's Trial, Lost
City State Park (West Virginia), Skyline Drive, Stonewall Jackson's Headquarters,
General Sheridan's Headquarters.

Courtesy of Dixie Caverns, Virginia.

VIRGINIA

DIXIE CAVERNS, 5596 Highfields Road S.W., Roanoke. 10 miles south of Roanoke on U.S. 11, 460, and Interstate 81. Phone: 703-774-4445.

Dixie Caverns is well decorated, and contains a species of salamander found only in this cave and the immediate vicinity. It is known as the Dixie Salamander. The cave has been commercialized since 1922. Known as the "Wedding Bell," this magnificent canopy, with stalagmites growing on its top, is seen in the photograph. *Open* all year from 8:00 A.M. to 9:00 P.M. in summer, 8:00 A.M. to 5:00 P.M. in winter.

Guided tour: 30 to 45 minutes.

Rates: adults, $1.50; children, $0.75; group rates available.

On premises: restaurant, gift shop, camping, trailer camp, picnicking, grocery, and gas station. *Nearby:* all facilities.

Nearby attractions: Mill Mountain Children's Zoo, Blue Ridge Parkway, Wasena Transportation Museum, large amusement park, Roanoke, Organ Cave (West Virginia), Roanoke College, Virginia Polytechnic Institute, Radford College, Claytor Lake State Park, Booker T. Washington National Monument, Hollins College.

Courtesy of Endless Caverns, Virginia.

VIRGINIA

ENDLESS CAVERNS, New Market. On U.S. 11, 3 miles south of New Market. Take Interstate 81 exits #66 or 67. Phone: 703-422-3158.

Endless Caverns was discovered accidentally by two boys who chased a rabbit into a small hole beneath a rock. In the 1880's, shortly after the cave was discovered, dances were held in a great hall in the cave that became known as "Alexander's Ballroom," where fiddlers sat high upon a block of stone to play their music. At that time the cave was lighted by candles and magnesium flares on certain days called "illuminating days." A notable feature of Endless Caverns is the "Stone Age Room," a dining room operating at modest prices and decorated with murals, like those of the ancient cave art of Spain and France, by William Starkweather. There is also an exhibit of Starkweather's work in the Museum of Art on the premises. Interesting formations show several stalactites and stalagmites that have joined to form columns.
Open all year, from 8:00 A.M. to 6:00 P.M. September 15 to June 1, and from 8:00 A.M. to 8:00 P.M. June 1 to September 15.
Guided tour: 1¼ hours.
Rates: adults, $2.50; children 7 to 14, $1.00; group rates available.
On premises: restaurant, gift shop, camping, trailer camp, picnicking, lake with swimming, boating, and fishing. Art Museum.
Nearby: motels, baby sitters, and all facilities.
Nearby attractions: Luray Caverns, Shenandoah Caverns, Melrose Civil War Museum and Caverns, New Market Battlefield, Massanutten Caverns, Grand Caverns, Skyline Drive, Natural Chimneys, Lost River State Park (West Virginia), Big Meadows Park, Shenandoah National Park.

65

VIRGINIA

GRAND CAVERNS,
Grottoes. U.S. 340
and State Route 256,
about 5 miles east
of Route 11. Phone:
703-249-2451.

Courtesy of Grand Caverns, Virginia.

Grand Caverns is famous for its shield formations. It was originally called Weyer's Cave for its discoverer, Bernard Weyer, and some road signs still remain directing traffic to Weyer's Cave. Thomas Jefferson visited the cavern from his estate at Charlottesville, and it is historically confirmed that Stonewall Jackson quartered his troops in this large and well-decorated cave. The room shown in the photograph is known as "Cathedral Hall."

Open all year. From May 1 to September 15, 8:00 A.M. to 8:00 P.M.; balance of year, 9:00 A.M. to 5:00 P.M. only.

Guided tour: 1 hour and 10 minutes.

Rates: adults, $2.50; children 6 through 12, $1.00; groups of 15, adults, $1.25.

On premises: snack bar, gift shop, camping, picnicking. *Nearby:* restaurants, motels, hotels, cabins, trailer camp.

Nearby attractions: Natural Chimneys, Endless Caverns, Massanutten Caverns, Woodrow Wilson Birthplace, Home of Thomas Jefferson, Home of James Monroe, Shenandoah Caverns, Luray Caverns, Big Meadows Recreational Area, Brandywine Recreational Area, Hone Quarry Recreational Area, North River Recreational Area, Sherand Lake Recreational Area, University of Virginia, Shenandoah National Park, Blue Ridge Parkway, Mary Baldwin College.

Courtesy of Luray Caverns, Virginia.

VIRGINIA

LURAY CAVERNS, Box 389, Luray. Route U.S. 211, U.S. 340. Phone: 703-743-6551.

Luray Caverns was discovered in 1878, and has been continually open to the public from that year. It has a series of rooms connected by passageways radiating from a central space like the spokes of a wheel from the hub. These natural passages permit a tour without the retracing of any passage. The cave is replete with formations of every kind and size, and limpid pools of water. A major attraction in the cave is this Great Stalacpipe Organ, a musical instrument deriving its tone directly from stalactites in the cave. The beautiful musical tones are produced by striking the stalactite formations with cushioned hammers that are electronically controlled and played like an organ, either manually or automatically.

Open every day of the year.

Guided tours every 20 minutes, starting at 9:00 A.M. Last tour, November 1 through March 31, 5:00 P.M.; June 16 through Labor Day, 7:00 P.M.; balance of year, 6:00 P.M.

Rates: adults, $2.50; children 7 to 14, $1.00; under 7, free. Special rates in effect for Armed Service personnel, special parties (25 or more), Boy Scouts and Girl Scouts, and school-sponsored educational tours.

On premises: restaurant, snack bar, gift shop, camping, trailer camp, picnicking. Also Car and Carriage Caravan, an exhibition of 75 authentically restored cars, carriages, and costumes, and Luray Singing Tower, a carillon of 47 bells. *Nearby:* all facilities.

Nearby attractions: Endless Caverns, Shenandoah Caverns, New Market Battlefield, Massanutten Caverns, Grand Caverns, Skyline Drive, Natural Chimneys, Lost River State Park (West Virginia), Skyline Caverns, Shenandoah National Park.

Courtesy of Massanutten Caverns, Virginia.

VIRGINIA

MASSANUTTEN CAVERNS, Keezletown. From Harrisonburg take U.S. 33 to State 925. Turn north on 925 until it runs into State 620. Follow 620 past railroad tracks and school to Massanutten Cave Road. Phone: 703-269-2311.

Massanutten Caverns is named for the mountain peak nearby. In front of the cave is a large swimming pool which the owners say may be opened by the spring of 1966. The cave is well decorated, and there are no steps. Many types of formations can be found in the photograph of beautiful "King Solomon's Courtroom," including an unusual shield in the left center.

Open April to October, from 9:00 A.M. to 6:00 P.M. in summer, and on weekends in the spring and fall from 9:00 A.M. to 5:00 P.M.

Guided tours: 55 minutes.

Rates: adults, $1.90; children, $0.90. Group rates 20 or more: adults, $0.90; children, $0.60.

On premises: picnicking. *Nearby:* all facilities in Harrisonburg.

Nearby attractions: Endless Caverns, Luray Caverns, Shenandoah Caverns, New Market Battlefield, Grand Caverns, Skyline Drive, Natural Chimneys, Lost River State Park (West Virginia), Big Meadows Park, Shenandoah National Park.

VIRGINIA

**MELROSE
CAVERNS,**
Lacey Springs.
Directly on U.S. 11,
about 10 miles south
of New Market.
Phone:
703-434-7957.

Courtesy of Melrose Caverns, Virginia.

Melrose Caverns form what Lowell Thomas described as a "Civil War Memorial carved underground." It was here that General Frémont's army spent considerable time—time during which hundreds of his soldiers carved their names on the cave walls and columns, so that even today visiting relatives often find them. When these troops left the cave, they were severely beaten by Stonewall Jackson's troops, who then took over the cave and in turn left their names and initials carved in the limestone. The cave prides itself on its collection of Civil War relics housed in the Museum, an old stone building near the entrance. Also on display are the stove and other household utensils used in the Kennedy farmhouse where John Brown made his headquarters before his raid on Harpers Ferry. The relics have been authenticated. A large collection of Indian artifacts can also be seen. The "Diamond Cascade," so named because of the sparkle of the thousands of crystals in this spectacular formation, is seen in the photograph.

Open all year, from 9:00 A.M. to 5:00 P.M. October to June, and from 8:00 A.M. to 7:00 P.M. June to October.

Guided tour: 45 minutes.

Rates: adults, $1.30; children 7 to 12, $0.65. Museum: adults, $0.50; children, $0.25. Group rates available.

On premises: gift shop, picnicking, museum. *Nearby:* restaurant, motels, hotels, and all facilities on U.S. 11.

Nearby attractions: Endless Caverns, Luray Caverns, Shenandoah Caverns, New Market Battlefield, Massanutten Caverns, Grand Caverns, Skyline Drive, Natural Chimneys, Lost River State Park (West Virginia), Big Meadows Park, Shenandoah National Park.

Courtesy of Shenandoah Caverns, Virginia.

VIRGINIA

SHENANDOAH CAVERNS,
New Market. Off Interstate 81 and U.S. 11, about 4 miles north of New Market. Phone: 703-477-3115.

Shenandoah Caverns is the only cave in Virginia to provide elevator service to the tourist levels. The cave itself is well decorated and level, and wheelchairs and strollers can be taken on the tour. Shenandoah features tours timed to the needs of each visiting group so that those with less time to enjoy the beauties of the cave may get through more quickly. The cave is entered through the lobby of the Lodge, which contains many facilities.

Open all year, from 9:00 A.M. to 5:00 P.M. in fall and winter; from 9:00 A.M. to 6:00 P.M. in spring; and from 9:00 A.M. to 7:00 P.M. in summer.

Guided tours: from 1 to 1½ hours.

Rates: adults, $2.50; children 7 to 14, $1.00. Group rates: adults, $1.50; children, $0.75. Educational rates for Girl Scout and Boy Scout groups and school-sponsored groups: first to seventh grade, $0.50; eighth grade and above, $1.00.

On premises: snack bar, gift shop, picnicking. *Nearby:* restaurant, motels, hotels.

Nearby attractions: New Market Battlefield, Endless Caverns, Endless Caverns Museum, Luray Caverns, Melrose Caverns, Massanutten Caverns, Grand Caverns, Skyline Drive, Natural Chimneys, Lost River State Park (West Virginia).

Courtesy of Skyline Caverns, Virginia.

VIRGINIA

SKYLINE CAVERNS, Box 193, Front Royal. On U.S. 340, about 1 mile south of Front Royal. Phone: 703-635-4545.

Skyline Caverns has a unique story regarding its discovery. Walter S. Amos, of Winchester, Virginia, predicted the presence of a cave in the general locality by "scientific deduction." Following his predictions, excavation was made at the site of the present entrance, and the cave, containing a most unusual collection of anthodites, was revealed. The anthodite flowers were found in low, flat passageways deep in the cave. Careful excavation of the clay from the floor has permitted access to these beautiful formations.

Open all year, summer 8:00 A.M. to 8:00 P.M.; winter, 9:00 A.M. to 5:00 P.M.
Guided tour: 1 hour.
Rates: adults, $2.00; children (high school), $1.00; 7 to 12, $0.60.
On premises: gift shop, snack bar, picnicking. *Nearby:* restaurant, camping, motel, cabins, trailer camp.
Nearby attractions: Endless Caverns, Shenandoah Caverns, Luray Caverns, New Market Battlefield, Skyline Drive, Shenandoah National Park.

Courtesy of Organ Cave, West Virginia.

WEST VIRGINIA

ORGAN CAVE, Route 2, Box 186, Ronceverte. On State Route 63, about ½ mile off U.S. 219 and 5 miles off U.S. 60. Phone: 304-647-5551.

Organ Cave, known since 1704, is part of a large cave system extending for many miles. Thomas Jefferson visited the cave in 1778, and is reputed to have discovered and removed a complete skeleton, possibly of a dinosaur, which, it is claimed, is now in Baltimore, Maryland. The cave contains some of the country's best relics of saltpeter workings used during the Civil War. Of the original 52 hoppers, 37 remain and can be seen on the tour. The name Organ Cave comes from a large formation that distinctly resembles a church organ. The cave was opened to the public in 1900.

Open April to November, from 8:00 A.M. until all tourists are gone.

Guided tour: 1 hour.

Rates: adults, $1.00; children, $0.50, both plus tax. Group rates available.

On premises: gift shop, camping, picnicking. *Nearby:* restaurant, motels, hotel, cabins, trailer camp.

Nearby attractions: White Sulphur Springs, Old Rehobeth Church, Ponderosa Ranch, Coal House, Doll House, Kates Mountain Lookout Tower, National Fish Hatchery, Droop Mountain Battlefield, Watoga State Park, Donthan State Park, Dixie Caverns (Virginia), Blue Bend Recreation Area, Lake Sherwood, Greenbrier State Forest, resort areas.

Courtesy of Seneca Caverns, West Virginia.

WEST VIRGINIA

SENECA CAVERNS, Riverton. 3 miles from U.S. 33 at Riverton. Phone: 7F25 or 8F35.

Seneca Caverns once served as a refuge for the Seneca Indians. In fact, Chief Bald Eagle lived in the cave for a period. The caverns are 2,500 feet above sea level. Looking almost like flowing molasses, this flowstone wall is almost crystal white. *Open* April 1 to October 31, 8:00 A.M. to 8:00 P.M. daily.
Guided tour: 1 hour.
Rates: adults, $1.50; children, $0.75. Groups of 15 or more: adults, $1.00; children, $0.50.
On premises: restaurant, snack bar, gift shop, camping, trailer camp, picnicking.
Nearby: motels, hotel, cabins.
Nearby attractions: Smoke Hole Caverns, Sinks of Gandy, Shenandoah Caverns (Virginia), Endless Caverns (Virginia), Melrose Caverns (Virginia), Seneca Rocks, Blackwater Falls State Park, Lost River State Park, Spruce Knob (highest point in West Virginia), Spruce Knob Lake Recreation Area, Hone Quarry Recreation Area (Virginia), Natural Chimneys (Virginia), Stuart Recreation Area, Davis and Elkins College, Monongahela National Forest.

WEST VIRGINIA

SMOKE HOLE CAVERN,
Moorefield. West Virginia State Route 4 and Route 28, about 8 miles west of Petersburg.

Courtesy of Smoke Hole Cavern, West Virginia.

Smoke Hole Cavern received its name from the fact that the Seneca Indians used the cave for centuries as a place for smoking meat. During the Civil War it was used as a storage place for ammunition. Later the cave became a spot for making corn whiskey, and the old still, together with the jugs used for storing the finished product, can be seen as part of the tour. The cave was commercialized in 1939. A girl guide points out a portion of the cave blackened by carbon caused by Indians smoking meat in the cave.

Open April 1 to December 1 daily from 8:00 A.M. to 7:00 P.M.

Guided tour: 50 minutes.

Rates: adults, $1.50; children, $0.50.

On premises: restaurant, snack bar, gift shop. *Nearby:* camping, motel, hotel, cabins, trailer camp, picnicking.

Nearby attractions: Champ Rocks, Seneca Rocks, Blackwater Falls State Park, Lost River State Park, Davis and Elkins College, Stuart Recreation Area, Spruce Knob Lake, Shenandoah Caverns (Virginia), Endless Caverns (Virginia), Grand Caverns (Virginia).

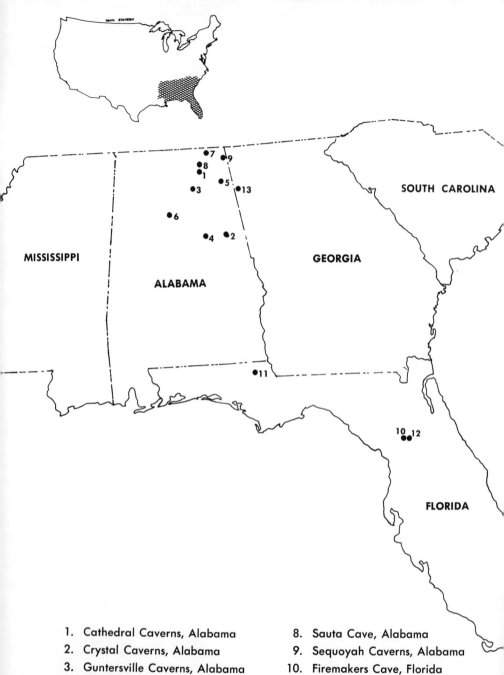

1. Cathedral Caverns, Alabama
2. Crystal Caverns, Alabama
3. Guntersville Caverns, Alabama
4. Kymulga Cave, Alabama
5. Manitou Cave, Alabama
6. Rickwood Caverns, Alabama
7. Russell Cave National Monument, Alabama

8. Sauta Cave, Alabama
9. Sequoyah Caverns, Alabama
10. Firemakers Cave, Florida
11. Florida Caverns, Florida
12. Ocala Caverns, Florida
13. Cave Springs Cave, Georgia

3. SOUTHEASTERN REGION

Alabama
Florida
Georgia
Mississippi
South Carolina

All the physical factors and environment necessary for the formation of a cave have to be present at the same time or this phenomenon does not develop. Florida has the climate, limestone, vegetation, and rainfall to make it one of the finest cave states (in numbers of caves), but it lacks the elevation. Hundreds of caves are still submerged beneath the coral cover in the lowlands of southern Florida. Many of these can be seen under the clear water in such places as Silver Springs. These have been entered by cave scuba divers, and many well-preserved fossil bones have been found in them. Only in the panhandle section of Florida are these caves elevated sufficiently to permit convenient entrance. In Alabama and Georgia, in the continuation of the limestone belt that cuts diagonally across the eastern United States, there are large and highly decorated caves to visit. In the Southeastern Region can be seen a variety of caves, ranging from the underwater caves in the crystal-clear springs of Florida, through the scenic stalagmitic caves in the northern part of the region, to the archaeological sites of early man in the United States dating back 8,000 years.

ALABAMA

CATHEDRAL CAVERNS, Grant. Just off U.S. 72, 431 and State Highway 79. Phone: 205-728-4722.

Courtesy of Cathedral Caverns, Alabama.

Cathedral Caverns has a huge entrance 125 feet wide and 50 feet high. The first chamber runs for several thousand feet before it is interrupted by breakdown. A stream runs through the first half of this well-decorated cave. Many artifacts have been found, some dating back thousands of years. On display are the bones of a prehistoric cave bear. The photo shows "Mighty Goliath," a huge stalagmite 60 feet tall and 200 feet around its base. It is on the edge of Mirror Lake.

Open all year, in summer from 8:00 A.M. to 6:00 P.M.; in spring and fall from 9:00 A.M. to 5:00 P.M.; and in winter from 10:00 A.M. to 4:00 P.M.

Guided tour: 1¼ hours.

Rates: adults, $1.75; children, age 5 through 12, $0.90. Groups of 15: adults, $1.25; children, $0.65.

On premises: snack bar, gift shop, overnight camping, picnicking. *Nearby:* restaurant, motels, hotel, cabins, trailer camp.

Nearby attractions: Huntsville Space Orientation Center and Museum, Guntersville Lake, Guntersville Dam, Guntersville Caverns, Manitou Cave, Sauta Cave, Ave Maria Grotto, Monte Sano State Park.

CRYSTAL CAVERNS, Clay. On Caverns Road, Clay, just off Old Springville Road (County 30). Phone: 205-664-9018.

Discovered in 1840, the cave was first commercialized in 1927. It has been previously known as Alabama Caverns, McClunney Cave, and Trussville Caverns. There are a waterfall and a spring in the lowest portion of the cave.

Open March through October, from 9:00 A.M. to 6:00 P.M.

Guided tour: 35 to 40 minutes.

Rates: adults, $1.00; children, $0.50. Group rates available.

On premises: snack bar, gift shop, camping, picnicking, nature trails. *Nearby:* motels.

Nearby attractions: Camp Cosby, Emerald Valley, Zamora Park, Horseshoe Bend National Military Park, Talladega College, Kymulga Caverns, marble quarries.

Note: a late report at press time indicates this cave may be closed.

Courtesy of Guntersville Caverns, Alabama.

ALABAMA

GUNTERSVILLE CAVERNS, Guntersville. 9 miles south of Guntersville on State Highway 79. Phone: 205-582-5575.

Guntersville Caverns has coined a name for its formations called "whosababies" —natural formations said to resemble people and animals, some of which can be seen in the photograph. Indian artifacts are on display.

Open all year, from 8:00 A.M. to 6:00 P.M. in summer and from 9:00 A.M. to 4:00 P.M. in winter.

Guided tour: 45 minutes.

Rates: 12 years and older, $1.50; 6 to 12, $0.75; under 6, free.

On premises: light refreshments, gift shop, camping, picnicking. *Nearby:* restaurant, snack bar, motels, hotels, cabins, trailer camp, picnicking, baby sitters, horseback riding, boat excursions.

Nearby attractions: Guntersville Lake, Ave Maria Grotto, Little Mountain State Park, Cathedral Caverns, Sauta Cave, Hurricane Creek Park, Noccalula Falls, Monte Sano State Park, Huntsville Space Orientation Center and Museum, Manitou Cave.

KYMULGA CAVE, Route 1, Childersburg. 5½ miles
east of Childersburg, 400 feet off State Highway 76.
Phone: 205-378-6956.

It is claimed that De Soto visited this cave in 1540. The cave undoubtedly has
an early history of visitation by others than Indians. In 1796, Benjamin Hawkins,
who was George Washington's Indian agent, visited the cave and gave a report
of it to Washington. The cave was commercialized in 1964. A large collection of
old histories and Indian trader maps is on display, together with many Indian relics.
Open all year.
Guided tour: 1 hour.
Rates: adults, $1.50; children 6 through 11, $0.75. Group rates available.
On premises: camping and picnicking. *Nearby:* in Childersburg, most facilities.
Nearby attractions: Crystal Caverns, Andrew Jackson's Fort Lashley, Talladega
College, Logan and -Martin lakes, Cheaha State Park (highest mountain in Ala-
bama), Lay Dam, Coosa (De Soto's Camp), marble quarries.

ALABAMA

MANITOU CAVE,
Fort Payne. 6 blocks
off U.S. 11 within city
limits of Fort Payne,
and 1 mile from
Interstate 59. Phone:
205-845-2881.

Courtesy of Manitou Cave, Alabama.

"Manitou" means "Great Spirit" in Cherokee Indian, and the cave was so named by the Indians, who considered it the home of a god who controlled the forces of nature. There are over 400 feet of steel bridges that span a crystal-clear underground stream. In 1889, Rainbow Lake was created by construction of a dam. In the 1890's, a 96-foot ballroom was built, where dancing was held by candlelight, and the dance floor remains to this day. Indian writing can be seen on the walls of the cave. Formed by drippings from the small stalactite on the ceiling, this large stalagmite known as the "Haystack," is seen in the photo.

Open all year, 8:00 A.M. to 5:00 P.M. daily. Extended hours in summer.

Guided tour: 45 minutes.

Rates: adults, $1.50; children 6 to 12, $0.75; under 6, free. Group rates (10 or more): adults, $0.75; children, $0.50.

On premises: gift shop, picnicking. The cave is 6 blocks from all other city facilities.

Nearby attractions: De Soto Canyon area, Sequoyah Cave, Cloudland Canyon (Georgia), Russell Cave National Monument, Sauta Cave, Cathedral Caverns, Guntersville Caverns, Little Mountain State Park, De Soto Falls area, Noccalula Falls, Berry College (Georgia).

ALABAMA

RICKWOOD CAVERNS, Warrior. 6 miles north of
Warrior on State Highway 31.

Rickwood Caverns is located in a 160-acre area. The cave contains pits and
domes, and it is not necessary to retrace steps on the ¾-mile tour through the cave.
Open all year, 8:00 A.M. until sunset.
Rates: not known. Scout groups are admitted free of charge.
On premises: playground, picnic area, hiking, Olympic-size swimming pool, restaurant. *Nearby:* all facilities in Birmingham.
Nearby attractions: Birmingham, Russell Cave National Monument, Robinson
Foundry (Alexander City), University of Alabama Museum of Natural History
(Tuscaloosa), Muscle Shoals, Crystal Caverns, Cathedral Caverns.

RUSSELL CAVE NATIONAL MONUMENT, Bridgeport. U.S. 72 to County Road 91, then north to Mount
Carmel, then right turn on County Road 75 to entrance. Phone: 205-495-2672.

Russell Cave National Monument was established in 1961. Some 310 acres, a
gift of the National Geographic Society, were set aside for protection of the site
and its surroundings. This monument is of interest to archaeologists. Visitors are
permitted exploration of the cave itself only with special permission, as it is large
and completely undeveloped. The exhibits in the visitors' center were taken from
the excavation inside the cave entrance. Artifacts found in the cave date back as
far as 8,000 years. The archaeological excavation inside the cave entrance is interpreted by a miniature sound-and-light program.
Open all year, in summer from 8:00 A.M. to 6:00 P.M.; in winter until 5:00 P.M.
Self-guided tour to archaeological site only, well lighted.
Rates: no charge.
On premises: picnicking only. *Nearby:* restaurant, snack bar, motels, hotel, baby
sitters.
Nearby attractions: Cathedral Cave, Sauta Cave, Sequoyah Cave, Manitou Cave,
Chattanooga, Lookout Mountain, Lookout Mountain Cave and Ruby Falls, Rock
City, Crystal Cave, and many other attractions.

Courtesy of Sauta Cave, Alabama. Photo by William Varnedoe.

ALABAMA

SAUTA CAVE, Scottsboro. 10 miles west of Scottsboro on U.S. 72, then 5 miles east on Jackson County paved road No. 11. Phone will be installed when cave is open.

This cave is expected to be open in the fall of 1966. It is on two levels, the lower containing a small stream. The plans for development include a stagecoach ride from the lower to the upper entrance and a boat ride out of the lower level. The cave was the scene of saltpeter workings during the War of 1812 and the Civil War. These workings will be on view for tourists. Tape-recorded lectures will be given at each point of historic interest. This VW bus travels the route of the old mule-drawn mine carts. A feature on the tour will be the "Underground Grand Canyon" section of the cave.

Open all year, from 8:00 A.M. to 6:00 P.M.

Guided tour from 60 to 75 minutes.

Rates: adults, $2.00; children, $1.00. Group rates available.

On premises (planned): restaurant, snack bar, gift shop, camping, picnicking, swimming, fishing. Long-term plans include cabins and trailer camp. *Nearby:* motels.

Nearby attractions: Huntsville Space Orientation Center and Museum, Guntersville Lake, Guntersville Dam, Guntersville Caverns, Manitou Cave, Sequoyah Cave, Russell Cave National Monument, Widows Creek Steam Plant, Little Mountain State Park, Monte Sano State Park.

NOTE: Though all information is tentative, it is the latest available at the time of printing.

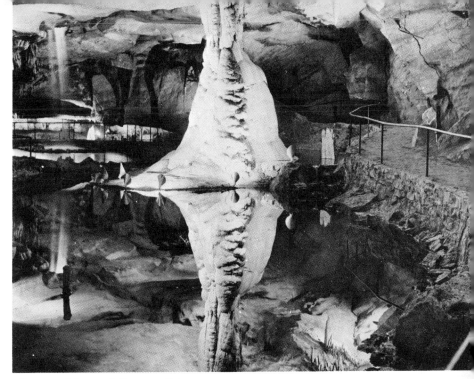

Courtesy of Sequoyah Caverns, Alabama.

ALABAMA

SEQUOYAH CAVERNS, Valley Head. Off U.S. 11 and Interstate 59, about 35 miles south of Chattanooga, Tennessee. Phone 205-635-5779.

Formerly known as Ellis Cave, Sequoyah Caverns opened in 1964. The cave is named in honor of Sequoyah, the famous Cherokee Indian who invented the only written alphabet of the Cherokee language. His name is also perpetuated by the "Sequoia" trees of California. Chief Sequoyah lived and taught in the cave area. One of the features of the cave, seen on the left, is a waterfall that enters through the roof and descends to the floor.

Open all year, from 7:00 A.M. to 6:00 P.M. in summer, and from 8:00 A.M. to 4:00 P.M. in winter.

Guided tour: 1 hour.

Rates: adults, $1.50; children, $0.75. Groups: adults, $0.75; children, $0.50.

On premises: gift shop, camping, picnicking, lounge. *Nearby:* restaurants, snack bar, motels, trailer camp.

Nearby attractions: De Soto Falls, Sauta Cave, Guntersville Caverns, Manitou Cave, Lookout Mountain, Ruby Falls Cave, Guntersville Lake and Dam, De Soto State Park and Canyon Area, Weiss Reservoir, Russell Cave, Cathedral Caverns.

FIREMAKERS CAVE

THIS CAVE WAS DISCOVERED THROUGH A SO-CALLED POTHOLE OR NATURAL WELL IN THE ROOF. PARTIALLY FILLED WITH SAND AND CLAY. FURTHER EXPLORATION DISCLOSED A SPACIOUS CORRIDOR WITH A CATHEDRAL CHAMBER WHOSE VAULTED CEILING REVEALS THE SOOT FROM FIRES OF PREHISTORIC MAN.

Courtesy of Firemakers Cave, Florida.

FLORIDA

FIREMAKERS CAVE, Ocala.

A small cave operated in conjunction with Ocala Caverns. Admission to Ocala Caverns includes admission to Firemakers Cave. See Ocala Caverns for details.

FLORIDA

FLORIDA CAVERNS,
Florida Caverns State Park, P.O. Box 447, Marianna. 3 miles north of Marianna on State Road 167. Phone: 904-482-3632.

Courtesy of Florida Caverns, Florida.
Photo by Florida News and Photo Service.

Discovered in 1937, Florida Caverns was opened to the public in 1942. While the lowest point on the tour is only 65 feet below the surface, the cave is actually developed on two levels, the upper level being permanently dry. The lower level is filled with water during flood periods. There are several artificial entrances, and tours are changed, using different entrances in accordance with the water levels. The cave is situated in the center of a well-developed state-operated recreational park. Florida Caverns has an immense, almost impenetrable forest of columns that creates a weird and unusual effect.
Open all year, from 7:00 A.M. to 7:00 P.M. (Sundays and holidays opening time is 8:00 A.M.).
Guided tour: 45 minutes.
Rates: adults, $1.50; children, $0.25. Group rates available. There is a $0.50-per-car charge for park entry.
On premises: snack bar, gift shop, camping, trailer camp, picnicking, golf course, swimming, boating, water sports. *Nearby:* restaurant, hotels, motels, cabins.
Nearby attractions: Falling Waters State Park, Battle of Marianna State Historical Memorial, Three Rivers State Park, Lake Seminole, Seminole State Park (Georgia), Chattahoochee State Park (Alabama).

Courtesy of Ocala Caverns, Florida.

FLORIDA

OCALA CAVERNS, Route 2, Box 182Y, Ocala. 8 miles south of Ocala on U.S. 441-301-27. Phone: 904-245-3011.

Advertised as the "Home of Santa Claus," Ocala Caverns features the "Hall of Fame of Wrestling," since the cave is operated by Man Mountain Dean, Jr., who weighs 628 pounds. Ocala Caverns itself consists of a boat ride, the starting point of which is shown here. Entry fee also includes admission to Firemakers Cave, a small cave on the property.

Open all year, 9:00 A.M. to 9:00 P.M. daily.

Guided tour: 45 minutes (two caves).

Rates: adults, $1.00; children, $0.50.

On premises: gift shop, picnicking, rock display, Man Mountain Dean, Jr., and Violet Ray (World's Woman Lightweight Wrestling Champion). *Nearby:* Florida resort areas with all facilities.

Nearby attractions: Six Gun Territory, Silver Springs, Rainbow Springs, Rainforest, Cook's Buffalo Ranch, Silver Glen Springs, Juniper Springs recreation area, Ocala National Forest, orange groves, horse farms, 3,000 lakes, floating islands.

CAVE SPRINGS CAVE, Cave Spring, Floyd County.
Near junction of U.S. 411 and State Highway 100.

The cave contains a water passage that has not been completely explored. The commercialized portion of the cave also contains a stream up to 6 inches deep, and visitors may traverse the cave passage barefooted, as the stream has a sandy bottom and walking is comfortable.

Open all year.

Self-guided: bring lights.

Rates: $0.25 per person.

On premises: food stand. *Nearby:* all facilities in Rome.

Nearby attractions: Berry College, Red Top Mountain State Park, George Washington Carver State Park, Allatoona Lake, Manitou Cave (Alabama), Atlanta Campaign Historical Site, Weiss Reservoir (Alabama), De Soto Canyon State Park Recreation Area.

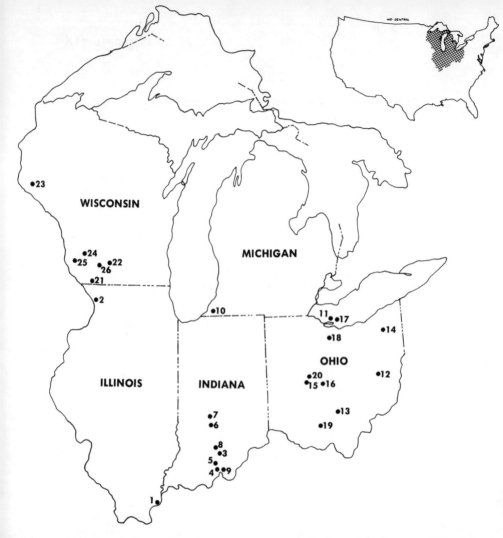

1. Cave-in-Rock, Illinois
2. Mississippi Palisades State Park, Illinois
3. Cave River Valley Park, Indiana
4. Little Wyandotte Cave, Indiana
5. Marengo Cave, Indiana
6. McCormick's Creek State Park, Indiana
7. Porter's Cave, Indiana
8. Spring Mill State Park, Indiana
9. Wyandotte Caverns, Indiana
10. Bear Cave, Michigan
11. Crystal Cave, Ohio
12. Devil's Den Park, Ohio
13. Hocking Hills State Parks, Ohio
14. Nelson's Ledges, Ohio
15. Ohio Caverns, Ohio
16. Olentangy Caverns, Ohio
17. Perry's Cave, Ohio
18. Seneca Caverns, Ohio
19. Seven Caves, Ohio
20. Zane Caverns, Ohio
21. Badger Mine, Wisconsin
22. Cave of the Mounds, Wisconsin
23. Crystal Cave, Wisconsin
24. Eagle Cave, Wisconsin
25. Kickapoo Caverns, Wisconsin
26. Lost River Cave, Wisconsin

4. MID-CENTRAL REGION

Illinois
Indiana
Michigan
Ohio
Wisconsin

The Great Lakes region suffered the same battering of the glaciers as the New England region. The enormous weight of the ice depressed the land, creating the Great Lakes and the elaborate drainage system of the region. The resulting caves left from this inundation do not have the size of those just to the south of this area. What they lack in size they often make up in unusual formations. Pure white stalactites and calcite crystals, as well as rimstone pools, are quite common in these caves. Mining of gypsum and epsom salts was done by the Indians; and evidences of their existence, dating back 4,000 years, have been found. Some caves were discovered during later mining operations for lead and zinc, and display fine examples of crystalline growth.

Courtesy of Cave-in-Rock State Park, Illinois. Photo by George Jackson.

ILLINOIS

CAVE-IN-ROCK, Cave-in-Rock State Park, Cave-in-Rock. State Route 1 on Ohio River 40 miles southwest of Evansville, Indiana. Phone: 618-289-2401.

Known to white men since the early 1700's, this cave has a bloody history unequaled perhaps by any other cave in the world. It was used as headquarters for pirates on the Ohio River, as a counterfeiting center, as dens for robbers and murderers, including the infamous Samuel Mason and the even more infamous Harpe brothers. Its huge entrance, shown here, borders the Ohio River where it commands a view of the river traffic, which asset the river pirates used to great advantage.
Open all year, 7:30 A.M. to 10:00 P.M.
Self-guided tour: large cave entrance lights most of the cave in daylight. Bring lights for night exploration.
Rates: free.
On premises: camping, trailer camp, picnicking, food concession operated during season. *Nearby:* restaurant, snack bar, gift shop, motels.
Nearby attractions: Fluorspar mines, Shawnee-town, Lake Glendale Beach and Picnic Ground, Dam Village (Kentucky), Wabash River, Ohio River.

Courtesy of Illinois Information Service. Photo by Division of Parks, Springfield, Illinois.

ILLINOIS

MISSISSIPPI PALISADES STATE PARK, P.O. Box 364, Savanna. State Route 84 on Mississippi River, 3 miles north of Savanna. Phone: 815-273-2731.

This park has two caves, Bob Upton Cave and Bat Cave; neither one is of great size but both are of historical interest in the region. Bob Upton, for whom the larger cave was named, was a resident of the area. In 1832, at the outbreak of the Black Hawk War, the settlers sent the women and children to Galena for safety, while the men remained to work the crops. One day a band of Indians appeared, and all the men except Upton fled to the river, where they had boats. Upton hid in the cave, and when the boats got opposite him he joined the other men. The cave has borne his name ever since. The cave entrance is in a bluff overlooking the Mississippi River. *Open* all year, daylight hours.

Self-guided tour: follow trail signs in the park. No lights necessary.

Rates: no charge.

On premises: camping, trailer camp, picnicking. *Nearby:* restaurant, motels.

Nearby attractions: Charles Mound, Apple River Canyon, Lake Le-Aqua-Na, Grant Home.

INDIANA

CAVE RIVER VALLEY PARK, Campbellsburg. 2 miles north of State Route 60 at Campbellsburg. Phone: 812-653-3757.

Cave River Valley Park is a community-service project of Banner Publications Newspapers. The park contains 8 known caves for which entry permission must be obtained at the cabin office. None are lighted except the front part of River Cave. This cave is large, and requires a boat and several hours to explore; Endless Cave requires 2 or 3 hours, but the first ⅔ of it are easy walking. Bear Den Cave is very small but a good place to search for arrowheads. Dorsey is virtually unexplored. Crystal Spring Cave starts as a crawl, and is unexplored. Lake Cave is small and wet. Frozen Waterfall Cave needs two ropes for easy exploration. By far the most beautiful, Lamplighter's Cave takes 2 or 3 hours to explore. Be sure to get information as to which caves might flash-flood.

Open all year, 24 hours daily.

No guides: lights required in all caves.

Rates: admission to park (including caves), $0.15 per person plus $0.10 per car.

On premises: restaurant, snack bar, gift shop, camping, cabins, trailer camp, picnicking, fishing, boating, grist mill, 150-year-old cabin. *Nearby:* scattered facilities.

Nearby attractions: Spring Mill State Park (caves), Marengo Cave, Wyandotte Caves, Devils Back Bone, French Lick Mineral Springs, Brown County State Park, Lake Greenwood, Indiana University, Lawrence County Museum, Avoca State Fish Hatchery, Yellow Wood State Forest, Monroe Reservoir.

LITTLE WYANDOTTE CAVE, Wyandotte.

This cave is owned and operated by Wyandotte Caverns, and is used for the 45-minute tour in Wyandotte Caverns. See Wyandotte Caverns for details.

Courtesy of Marengo Cave, Indiana.

INDIANA

MARENGO CAVE, Marengo. ¼ mile off State Highway 64 in Marengo. Phone Marengo 10-2.

Marengo Cave was actually discovered, in 1883, by two children, a sister and a brother who followed an opening that led them 123 feet from the surface into the cave. It was opened commercially that same year. Marengo is noted for its colorful formations. The cave is quite level after an entry of 21 steps. Seen in the photo, this exquisite canopy formation is almost symmetrically formed.

Open March 1 through November, 9:00 A.M. to 5:00 P.M. daily.

Guided tour: 1 hour and 10 minutes.

Rates: adults, $1.85; children, $0.90. Group rates (10 or more): adults, $0.90; children, $0.75.

On premises: gift shop, picnicking, baby sitters (sometimes). *Nearby:* motel, limited facilities.

Nearby attractions: Wyandotte Cave, Little Wyandotte Cave, Spring Mill State Park and caves, Cave River Valley Caves, Corydon (first state capital), New Albany National Cemetery, Louisville and Fort Knox (Kentucky), French Lick Mineral Springs, Devils Back Bone, Ohio River.

INDIANA

PORTER'S CAVE
Paragon. State
Route 67. Phone:
317-879-3386.

Courtesy of Porter's Cave, Indiana.

Porter's Cave is renowned for its picturesque entrance halfway up a limestone bluff. Note the attractive waterfall formed by water from the cave. The cave has been owned by the same family for over 100 years, and the grandfather of the present owner operated a water mill just below the cave in 1816. The cave was commercialized in 1957.

Open May 1 to November 1 daily, 9:00 A.M. to 7:00 P.M.

Self-guided tour: bring your own lights.

Rates: $0.25 per person regardless of age.

On premises: snack bar, gift shop, camping, cabins (church camp), trailer camp, picnicking. *Nearby:* restaurant, motels.

Nearby attractions: Leiber State Park, Cataract Lake, McCormick Creek State Park, Indiana University, De Pauw University, Franklyn College, Cagles Mill State Park and Dam, Brown County State Park, Yellow Wood State Forest, Monroe Reservoir, goldfish hatchery.

SPRING MILL STATE PARK, Mitchell. On State Highway 60, east of Mitchell. Phone: Mitchell, Indiana, 129.

Spring Mill State Park contains a number of interesting caves. Donaldson Cave is noted for its blind fish deep in the cave, although they cannot be seen on the tourist trip. Visitors enter the cave by boat, going a short distance to an impressive waterfall. Twin Caves is also entered by boat but for a greater distance; the cave continues for another mile. Hamer's Cave furnishes the water that drives the Old Grist Mill in the Pioneer Village in the park.

Open April through October, 9:00 A.M. to 5:00 P.M. daily.

Guided tours.

Rates: $0.25 per person per cave.

On premises: restaurant, snack bar, gift shop, camping, inn, cabins, trailer camp, picnicking, Pioneer Village, Old Grist Mill, swimming, fishing, nature trails, boating, horseback riding, naturalist service in summer, playground, museum. *Nearby:* scattered facilities.

Nearby attractions: Cave River Valley Caves, Marengo Cave, Wyandotte Cave, Devils Back Bone, Brown County State Park, Lake Greenwood, French Lick Mineral Springs, Indiana University, Lawrence County Museum, Avoca State Fish Hatchery, Yellow Wood State Forest, Monroe Reservoir.

WOLF CAVE, McCormick's Creek State Park, Spencer. On State Highway 46, about 2 miles east of Spencer. Phone: 812-829-3947.

At the northern end of 1,225-acre McCormick's Creek State Park is Wolf Cave, a small cave open to visitors. On one side of it is a natural bridge. Another cave on the property is known as Sunken Cave.

Open all year, 7:00 A.M. to 11:00 P.M.

Self-guided tour: flashlights required.

Rates: admission to park, $0.20 per person and $0.35 per vehicle. No charge for cave visit.

On premises: restaurant, snack bar, gift shop, camping, hotel, primitive cabins, trailer camp, picnicking, naturalist service, swimming pool, horseback riding, nature trails, playground, sports fields, trailside museum, campfire programs, stone quarry (winter facilities limited). *Nearby:* motel, other facilities in Spencer.

Nearby attractions: Indiana University, Brown County State Park, De Pauw University, Cagles Mill State Park and Dam, Cataract Lake, Yellow Wood State Forest, Monroe Reservoir, Lieber State Park, Franklyn College, Porter's Cave, goldfish hatchery.

INDIANA

**WYANDOTTE
CAVERNS,**
Wyandotte. On U.S.
460 and State
Highway 62, about
35 miles west of
Louisville, Kentucky.
Phone: 812-738-2782
or 812-633-4341.

*Courtesy of Wyandotte Caverns, Indiana.
Photo by George Jackson.*

It is believed that Indians penetrated farther into Wyandotte Caverns than into any other cave. Normally, Indians did not go beyond daylight in caves, but far back in Wyandotte a natural auditorium containing this huge stalagmite was used as a ceremonial room. Hickory torches and remnants of ceremonial fireplaces have been found there. Indians also obtained flint from the cave for barter and for arrow and spearheads. The flint quarry can still be seen. Wyandotte was also mined extensively during the War of 1812 for the saltpeter used in making gunpowder. Wyandotte Caverns is famous for its huge stone mountains, rising as high as 175 feet in sections of the cave. The cave has over 23 miles of passage.

Open April through September from 9:00 A.M. to 5:00 P.M.

Guided tour: 45 minutes to 8 hours.

Rates: adults (45-minute tour), $1.50; (2-hour tour), $2.00; (5-hour tour), $4.00; (8-hour tour), $5.00; children, half of adult price.

NOTE: The 45-minute tour is in *Little Wyandotte Cave,* a small, but beautiful adjoining cave.

On premises: restaurant (in season only), gift shop, camping, motel, cabins, trailer camping, picnicking. The cave operates a lodge, motel, and cabins. *Nearby:* all facilities.

Nearby attractions: Corydon, first capital of Indiana, Harrison County State Forest, Lincoln Memorial, Spring Mill State Park and Caves, Bedford Stone Mills, French Lick Mineral Springs, Santa Claus, Fort Knox (Kentucky), Marengo Cave, Cave River Valley Caves, Ohio River, New Albany National Cemetery.

MICHIGAN

BEAR CAVE, Rural Route 1, Box 550, Buchanan. 4 miles north of Buchanan on Red Bud Trail. Phone: 616-695-3050.

Now operated in connection with a resort and camp grounds, Bear Cave was a habitat of the Potawatomi Indians. An early movie thriller, *The Great Train Robbery,* used Bear Cave as the cache in which the train robbers hid their loot.
Open April 1 to November 1, 9:00 A.M. to 6:00 P.M. Memorial Day through Labor Day. Open weekends only during balance of season.
Guided tour: approximately 15 minutes.
Rates: 6 years and up, $0.50; under 6 years, $0.25; babes in arms, free.
On premises: gift shop, camping, trailer camp, picnicking, playground, boating, fishing. *Nearby:* restaurant, motels, hotels, cabins.
Nearby attractions: Lake Michigan, Warren Dunes State Park, Andrews University, Notre Dame University (Indiana), Paw Paw Lake, House of David, Fort St. Joseph Museum, Little Fish Lake, Pleasant Lake, Carey Lake, Deer Forest, Storyland Zoo (Indiana), Lake Chapin.

OHIO

CRYSTAL CAVE, South Bass Island, Put-in-Bay. South Bass Island is reached by ferry from Port Clinton on State Highway 2. Phone: 419-285-2811.

Crystal Cave, located on the property of the Heineman Winery and Vineyards, is unusual in that a solid mass of strontium crystals covers much of the interior of the cave. These crystals have 10 faces, and the angle of each face on one crystal is exactly the same degree as that on the like face of every other crystal. The crystals are the world's largest. This deposit of strontium sulfate is the only one of any size in the U.S. It was discovered in 1897 when a well was dug in search of water for domestic purposes.
Open from May 30 through Labor Day, 9:00 A.M. to 5:00 P.M.
Rates: adults, $0.35; children, $0.20.
On premises: restaurant, snack bar, lunch room, hotel, cabins, camping. *Nearby:* scattered facilities.
Nearby attractions: Perry's Cave, Seneca Caverns, Perry Memorial National Monument, Blue Hole, Kellys Island State Park, Catawba Island State Park, East Harbor State Park, Cedar Point, Crave Creek State Park, Birthplace of Thomas Edison, other islands.

Courtesy of Devil's Den Park, Ohio.

OHIO

DEVIL'S DEN PARK, R.D. 2, Tippecanoe. Take County
Route 10 out of Gnadenhutten and follow signs to
park. Phone: 614-498-7254.

There are several caves and rock shelters in this park, of which the best known are Devil's Den and Wetzel Cave. The legend of Devil's Den and Lewis Wetzel, for whom the cave is named, is told in Zane Grey's book *The Spirit of the Border,* Shown here is one of the geological wonders of the park, the overhanging rocks.
Open May 1 to October 1, dawn to dusk.
Self-guided tours: flashlights required.
Rates: adults, $0.50; children, $0.25 (includes swimming and all recreational activities).
On premises: refreshments, gift shop, camping, cabins, trailer camping, picnicking, trails, playground, sports. *Nearby:* restaurant (8 miles), motel (10 miles).
Nearby attractions: Gnadenhutten Monuments, Gnadenhutten Museum, Schoenbrunn State Park, Muskingum Watershed Lakes, Fort Laurens State Park, Zoar Village and Gardens, U.S. Hydrologic Lake State Park, Belmont State Park, Wills Creek Reservoir, Clendening Reservoir, Piedmont Reservoir, Tappen Dam, Warther Museum.

HOCKING HILLS STATE PARKS, Route 2, Logan. A series of state parks near Logan, Ohio, spread over approximately a 5-by-10-mile area best entered at junctions of state routes 374 and 56. Phone: 614-385-4402.

In a beautiful setting, these parks have many scenic attractions, including waterfalls and 3 caves open to the public. Ash Cave, while small, is known for its acoustical perfection, which magnifies even the slightest sounds. The cave contains ashes of fires believed to have been kindled by Ohio's early settlers, hence the name. Old Man's Cave is more of a gorge than a cave, and includes interesting vegetation and cascades. Rock House is situated in a cliff that reaches upward for 150 feet. Halfway up, large pillars of weathered sandstone grace the cave entrance in a variety of colors. The cave has 7 passageways, and is reputed to have been used as a shelter for Indians, a cache for horse thieves, and a hideaway for fugitives.

Open all year, daylight to dark.

Self-guided tour: 1 to 3 hours.

Rates: no charge.

On premises: gift shop, camping, trailer camp, picnicking, hiking. *Nearby:* scattered facilities.

Nearby attractions: A. W. Marion State Park, Tar Hollow State Park, Scroto Trail State Park, Lake Alma State Park and Reservoir, Lake Hope State Park, Burr Oak State Park, Buckeye Lake State Park, Conkles Hollow State Park, Cedar Falls State Park, Mound City Group National Monument, Indian Mounds, Ross Historical Museum, Leo Petroglyphs.

OHIO

NELSON'S LEDGES,
R.F.D. 2, Box 292,
Garrettsville. State
Route 282 off U.S.
422, about 3 miles
east of Parkman.
Phone:
216-548-8348.

Courtesy of Nelson's Ledges, Ohio.

Nelson's Ledges is partly privately owned and partly in Nelson Ledge Kennedy State Park. It consists of an almost unbelievable mass of glacial boulder deposits over a mile in length. There are many small caves formed by the boulders, but the principal ones are Gold Hunter's Cave and Devil's Den. Note that the caves are often wet and slippery underfoot in the rainy season.

Open March 1 to November 7, 9:00 A.M. to dusk.

Self-guided tour: flashlights advisable in 2 main caves.

Rates: no charge for caves, but there may be a small entry free.

On premises: restaurant, snack bar, gift shop, camping, picnicking. *Nearby:* all facilities on U.S. 422.

Nearby attractions: Nelson Ledge Deer Park, amusements, Lake Erie cities and lakefront, including Cleveland; First Mormon Temple in U.S., McKinley Memorial, Garfield Birthplace, Hiram College, Kent State University, Punderson State Park, Mosquito State Park, Mosquito Creek Reservoir, many other lakes and reservoirs, Akron, Youngstown.

Courtesy of Ohio Caverns, Ohio.

OHIO

OHIO CAVERNS, RFD 1, West Liberty. On State Route 245 near West Liberty. Phone: 513-465-3227.

Ohio Caverns is noted for the many milk-white formations that look as though they have been hand polished. They protrude from the walls and floors of the cavern in ghostly contrast to the brown, mineral-stained walls. Sections of the cave have unusual helictite formations.

Open all year, 8:00 A.M. to 5:00 P.M.

Guided tour: 45 minutes to 1 hour.

Rates: adults, $1.55; children 8 through 14, $0.85; groups of 20 or more: adults, $0.85; children 8 through 14, $0.50.

On premises: gift shop, picnicking. *Nearby:* restaurant, camping, motels.

Nearby attractions: Zane Caverns, Olentangy Caverns, Mac-O-Chee Castle, Indian State Lake Park, Kiser Lake State Reservation, Richwood State Park, Indian fort and blockhouses, Wittenberg University.

Courtesy of Olentangy Caverns, Ohio.

OHIO

OLENTANGY CAVERNS, Route 4, Delaware. Off State 315, about 10 miles north of Columbus and 2 miles west of U.S. 23. Phone: 614-548-2165.

Olentangy Caverns was used in the early 1800's by Wyandotte Indian Chief Leatherlips and his braves as a workshop to make arrows and stone implements. The room shown was the "Indian Council Chamber." Hundreds of artifacts have been found in the cave, and many are on display in the gift shop. Three of the 4 cave levels are open to the public. The fourth level contains a river and a lake of undetermined size that may someday be open for tourists. The cave has been commercialized since 1935.

Open daily June, July, and August; weekends, April, May, September, and October. Daily 9:30 A.M. to 6:00 P.M.; Sundays 9:30 A.M. to 8:00 P.M.

Guided tour: 25 minutes.

Rates: adults, $0.90; children, $0.50. Group rates available.

On premises: gift shop, camping (76 campsites), picnicking, shelter house, playground. *Nearby:* hotels, motels.

Nearby attractions: Zane Caverns, Columbus Zoo, Ohio Caverns, O'Shaughnessey Reservoir, Hoover Reservoir, Playhouse on Green, stone grist mills, Delaware Lake State Park, Delaware Dam and Reservoir, Perkins Observatory, Leatherlips Monument, Ohio State University, Ohio Wesleyan University, Denison University, Otterbein College, Central College, Franklin University.

PERRY'S CAVE, South Bass Island, Put-in-Bay. South Bass Island is reached by ferry from Port Clinton on State Highway 2. Phone: 419-285-3496.

Perry's Cave is reputed to have been discovered by Commodore Oliver Hazard Perry in 1813. It is claimed that Perry used the cave to store ammunition and cannon before the Battle of Lake Erie, and that British prisoners were kept there after the battle. The cave is 208 feet long and 165 feet wide.

Open June, July, and August, 11:00 A.M. to 5:00 P.M.

Guided tour: 15 to 20 minutes.

Rates: adults, $0.50; children, $0.25. NOTE: Island can be reached by ferry. For schedule and rates, write Parker Boat Line, Inc., Put-in-Bay, Ohio, or phone 419-732-2800.

On premises: gift shop, picnicking. Also on island: restaurant, snack bar, gift shop, state park, camping, hotel, motel, cabins, trailer camp, picnicking, swimming, fishing.

Nearby attractions: Crystal Cave, Seneca Caverns, Perry Memorial National Monument, Blue Hole, Kellys Island State Park, Catawba Island State Park, East Harbor State Park, Cedar Point, Crave Creek State Park, Birthplace of Thomas Edison, other islands.

Courtesy of Seneca Caverns, Ohio.

OHIO

SENECA CAVERNS, Bellevue. 4 miles south of Bellevue, 2 miles off state routes 18 or 269 on Township Road 178. Phone: 419-482-5570.

Few caves are formed entirely by earthquakes, but Seneca Caverns apparently was entirely formed in this manner—leaving tumbling rocks and passages turning in every direction, as you can see pictured here. Evidence has also been found, in the form of an Indian rug needle, that the cave was visited by Indians 1,500 years ago. The cave was named after Seneca John, whose tribe occupied 15,000 acres nearby in the days of the early settlers. The cave is on several levels, and at the lowest, crystal-clear "Old Mist'ry," an underground river, can be seen. The river feeds Blue Hole, a great artesian spring 14 miles to the north. "Earthquake Attic" is the name of the room in the photograph.

Open daily 8:00 A.M. to 7:00 P.M. from May 31 to Labor Day and on weekends in May, September, and October.

Guided tour: 1 hour.

Rates: adults, $1.75; children 8 through 13, $0.75; under 8, free; groups of 10, special rates available.

On premises: gift shop, limited camping, picnicking, three trailer spaces. *Nearby:* restaurant, snack bar, motels, hotels, cabins, trailer camp.

Nearby attractions: Lagoon Deer Park, Rutherford B. Hayes Home, glacial grooves, prehistoric forest, Heidelberg College, Crystal Cave, Perry Memorial National Monument, Blue Hole, Kellys Island State Park, Catawba Island State Park, East Harbor State Park, Cedar Point, Crave Creek State Park, Birthplace of Thomas Edison.

SEVEN CAVES, Bainbridge. On U.S. 50, about 4 miles west of Bainbridge. Phone: 513-365-1283.

A beautiful park in the hills of Highland County contains a rugged area of deep gorges, waterfalls, and 7 caves that are illuminated with unique push-button lighting operated by the visitor without guides. The trails to the caves are cement walks with handrails, and take the visitor past cliffs, canyons, and waterfalls. Shelters are placed along the trail.

Open March 15 to November 15 during daylight.

Self-guided tour: no lights necessary.

Rates: adults, $1.25; children, $0.50.

On premises: restaurant, snack bar, gift shop, picnicking. *Nearby:* camping, motels, cabins, trailer camp.

Nearby attractions: Lake Rocky Fork, Devil's Den Park, Wilmington College, Rocky Fork State Park, Mound City Group National Monument, Lake White State Reservation, Adams Lake State Reservation, Pike State Park, Scioto Trail State Park, Cowan State Park, Ross Historical Museum, Indian mounds.

ZANE CAVERNS, Rural Route 2, Bellefontaine. U.S. 33 to State 540, 7 miles east of Bellefontaine. Phone: 513-592-6172.

The owners of Zane Caverns operate an animal park on the cave property. On display are buffalo, deer, etc. There are many Indian forts and blockhouses in the area. The cave itself is on 2 levels, and has been commercialized since 1926.

Open April 15 to November 1. Park and gift shop open 24 hours, cave 9:00 A.M. to 5:00 P.M., but later tours are available on request.

Guided tour: 30 to 45 minutes.

Rates: adults, $1.50; children 6 to 12, $0.75; group rates available.

On premises: animal game park, snack bar, gift shop, camping, trailer camp, picnicking, playground. *Nearby:* restaurant, motels, hotels, cabins.

Nearby attractions: Boating, swimming, Ohio Caverns, Olentangy Caverns, Indian State Lake Park, Kiser Lake State Park, Richwood State Park, Mac-O-Chee Castle, Indian forts and blockhouses.

WISCONSIN

BADGER MINE, Shullsburg. On State Highway 11 in
Shullsburg. Phone: 608-965-4468.

While Badger Mine is not a cave, it has many of the attractions of a cave. It is
operated by the La Fayette Association for Retarded Children, Inc., for the benefit
of retarded children. Actually, it is a lead mine that was first operated in 1827 and
that extends for miles beneath the city. The tourist route covers the main passage
for a half mile, and from it side tunnels and workings can be seen. The original
miners in the area were Winnebago Indians who mined for lead in the very early
1800's. There are also a park and museum operated in connection with the mine.
It was opened to the public in 1965.

Open May 1 to November 1, from 9:00 A.M. to 5:00 P.M.

Guided tour: 30 minutes.

Rates: adults, $1.00; 12 to 18 years, $0.50; under 12, $0.25. Group rates available.

On premises: gift shop, picnicking, swimming pool, tennis courts, football field,
baseball field, museum. *Nearby:* all facilities in Shullsburg.

Nearby attractions: Dickeyville Grotto, Lost River Cave, Governor Dodge State
Park, Swiss Villages, New Glarus Woods State Park, Wisconsin State College and
Institute of Technology, Charles Mound State Park (Illinois), Crystal Cave (Iowa),
Dubuque (Iowa).

WISCONSIN

CAVE OF THE MOUNDS,

Blue Mounds. 4 miles west of Mount Horeb on U.S. 18 and U.S. 151. Phone 608-437-3355.

Courtesy of Cave of the Mounds, Wisconsin.

Cave of the Mounds was accidentally discovered by a blast from quarrying operations in 1939. It was opened commercially a year later. Recent extensions have opened 4 new rooms to the public, making a total of 18 rooms on 2 levels. The cave is well decorated and is located on a 400-acre farm. Known as the "Ridge of Statuary" in the "Hall of Statues," one of these formations looks almost like a camel when seen in profile.

Open April 15 to October 15, from 9:00 A.M. to 5:00 P.M. in spring and fall and from 8:00 A.M. to 7:00 P.M. in summer.

Guided tour: 40 minutes.

Rates: not available.

On premises: snack bar, gift shop, picnicking. *Nearby:* camping, motels, hotels, cabins.

Nearby attractions: Little Norway, University of Wisconsin, Natural Bridge, Governor Dodge State Park, New Glarus Woods State Park, Blue Mounds State Park, Lost River Cave, Eagle Cave, Badger Park Lead Mine, House on the Rock.

Courtesy of Crystal Cave, Wisconsin.

WISCONSIN

CRYSTAL CAVE,
Spring Valley. 1 mile
west of Spring
Valley on State
Highway 29. Phone:
715-778-4414.

Crystal Cave consists of a series of 33 rooms on 3 levels. Sections of the cave are lighted by ultraviolet "black light" to create weird and unusual color effects. Notice the double arch in the "Ball Room."
Open March 1 to November 1 from 9:00 A.M. to 6:00 P.M. in spring and fall and from 8:00 A.M. to 8:00 P.M. in summer.
Guided tours: complete tour 1½ hours, partial tour 45 minutes.
Rates: complete tour, adults, $1.75; children, $0.90. Partial tour, adults, $1.25; children, $0.60.
On premises: restaurant, children's playground, gift shop, camping, picnicking.
Nearby: motels.
Nearby attractions: House of Memories Museum, Spring Valley Dam (under construction in early 1966), fishing, swimming, Cedar Lake, Wisconsin State College, Lake Pepin, Stout State College, Lake Tainter.

WISCONSIN

EAGLE CAVE,
Route 2. Blue River.
Off Route 60, about
5 miles northwest of
Muscoda. Phone:
608-537-2446.

Courtesy of Eagle Cave, Wisconsin.

Eagle Cave was completely rejuvenated in the spring of 1964, with new colored lighting and picnicking inside the cave. The surrounding wild area has been transformed into a recreational area for summer and winter activities. There is dancing 3 nights a week in the cave. The photograph shows the onyx formations in the cave.
Open all year, from 7:00 A.M. to 9:00 P.M.
Guided tour: 1 hour.
Rates: adults, $1.50; teen-agers, $0.75; children 6 to 12, $0.50; under 6, free; groups of 20, $0.50.
On premises: snack bar, gift shop, camping, trailer camp, picnicking, swimming, fishing, baby sitters, dancing, play areas, games, horseback riding, trail hikes. In winter, sleigh rides, tobogganing and ice skating. *Nearby:* restaurant, motels, hotels, cabins.
Nearby attractions: House on the Rock, Wisconsin Dells, Prairie du Chien, Tower Hill State Park, Gay Mills State Orchard, Natural Rock Bridge, Frank Lloyd Wright Estate, Kickapoo Caverns, Lost River Cave, Governor Dodge State Park.

WISCONSIN

KICKAPOO CAVERNS, Wauzeka. On State Highway 60, about 16 miles southeast of Prairie du Chien. Phone: 608-875-5223.

The word Kickapoo is from the Indian (central Algonquin) Kiwigapawa, which French explorers translated to Quincapous. The word means "moving about" or "flitting." Kickapoo Caverns was discovered by lead miners in the early 1880's, and evidence of their work was found in the cave. Prior to opening the cave commercially in 1947, many Indian artifacts were found.

Open May 1 to October 31, spring and fall from 8:00 A.M. to 6:00 P.M., and in summer 8:00 A.M. to 8:00 P.M.

Guided tour: 45 minutes.

Rates: adults, $1.25; children 6 to 11, $0.60, all plus state tax.

On premises: gift shop, camping. *Nearby:* restaurant, snack bar, camping, motels, hotel, cabins, trailer camp, picnicking, baby sitters.

Nearby attractions: Phetteplace Museum, Villa Louis, Medical Museum, Rose Park Zoo, Moody's Museum, Spook Cave (Iowa), Mississippi Dams.

WISCONSIN

LOST RIVER CAVE,
25 West Main Street,
Madison. On U.S.
18, about 5 miles
west of Mount Horeb
at foot of Blue
Mounds State Park.
Phone:
608-256-0574.

Courtesy of Lost River Cave, Wisconsin.

Lost River Cave was largely formed by an underground river, and has 4 levels. Two new areas have been explored and may be opened to the public, but a large portion of the cave is still undeveloped. Pictured here are the massive onyx formations at the beginning of the second level.

Open June 1 through September, from 9:00 A.M. to 6:00 P.M.

Guided tour: ½ hour.

Rates: adults, $0.85; children, $0.40; group rates for 10 or more.

On premises: snack bar, gift shop. *Nearby:* restaurant, motels, hotel, cabins, trailer camp, picnicking.

Nearby attractions: Little Norway, Blue Mounds State Park, Cave of the Mounds, Norway Basin, Natural Bridge, Eagle Cave, Badger Park Lead Mine, Swiss Village, University of Wisconsin, Madison (state capital), New Glarus Woods State Park, Lake Waubesa, Governor Dodge State Park.

1. Crystal Lake Cave, Iowa
2. Maquoketa Caves, Iowa
3. Spook Cave, Iowa
4. Wonder Cave, Iowa
5. Minnesota Caverns, Minnesota
6. Mystery Cave, Minnesota
7. Niagara Cave, Minnesota
8. John Brown's Cave, Nebraska
9. Robber's Cave, Nebraska
10. Bethlehem Cave, South Dakota
11. Jewel Cave National Monument, South Dakota

12. Nameless Cave, South Dakota
13. Rushmore Cave, South Dakota
14. Sitting Bull Crystal Caverns, South Dakota
15. Stage Barn Crystal Cave, South Dakota
16. Thunder Head Falls, South Dakota
17. Wild Cat Cave, South Dakota
18. Wind Cave National Park, South Dakota
19. Wonderland Cave, South Dakota

5. NORTH CENTRAL REGION

Iowa
Kansas
Minnesota
Nebraska
North Dakota
South Dakota

In 1839, parts of this region were recognized as an important mineral area. A survey of Iowa, Wisconsin, and part of Illinois was made at that time to define the potential for the mining of lead and zinc. This geologic study shaped the development of the area and precipitated the land rush that resulted in a close inspection of the underground potential. Many caves were discovered during this period, some of them still open to the public today as notable examples. Features of the caves of this area include boxwork, dogtooth spar, selenite crystals, and moon milk. In Iowa and parts of Minnesota, lead miners broke into many caves. In South Dakota the discovery of gold caused every opening in the ground to be investigated, and the exploration of the caves became an important part of the gold-rush fever.

IOWA

CRYSTAL LAKE CAVE, Rural Route 3, Dubuque. U.S. 52 and U.S. 67, about 5 miles south of Dubuque. Phone: 319-582-4038.

Crystal Lake Cave was discovered in 1880 by a group of lead miners who drilled 40 feet into the ground and uncovered the cave. It has formations and a small crystal-clear lake. It was commercialized in 1932.

Open daily May 1 to Labor Day. After Labor Day to November 1 open weekends only, 8:00 A.M. to 6:00 P.M.

Guided tour: 35 minutes.

Rates: adults, $1.20; children 6 to 12, $0.60; under 6, free.

On premises: snack bar, gift shop, camping, picnicking. *Nearby:* all facilities.

Nearby attractions: Maquoketa Cave and State Park, Bellevue State Park, Wapsipinicon State Park, Trappist Monastery, St. Donatus (French village), Mississippi River Boat Rides, Clarke College, University of Dubuque, Laras College, Grant Home (Illinois), Mississippi Palisades State Park and Caves (Illinois), Dewey Memorial (Wisconsin), Badger Mine (Wisconsin).

MAQUOKETA CAVES, Maquoketa State Park, Maquoketa. State Route 130, about 6 miles northwest of Maquoketa. Phone: 319-Emeline-3251.

Maquoketa State Park contains 13 caves in an area of 192 acres. The caves are badly vandalized, souvenir hunters having robbed the caves of their rarest beauty, but some formations remain. All the caves are not lighted, although major caves are. Pathways to caves are marked.

Open all year, 8 hours daily.

Self-guided tour: bring lights, as all caves are not lighted.

Rates: free.

On premises: snack bar, gift shop, camping, trailer camp, picnicking, scenic trails.

Nearby: all facilities in city of Maquoketa.

Nearby attractions: Bellevue State Park, Wapsipinicon State Park, Trappist Monastery, St. Donatus (French village), Mississippi River boat rides, Clarke College, University of Dubuque, Laras College, Grant Home (Illinois), Mississippi Palisades State Park and Caves, Badger Mine (Wisconsin), Crystal Lake Cave.

IOWA

SPOOK CAVE,
McGregor. Off U.S.
Route 52, about 7
miles west of
McGregor.
Phone: McGregor,
Iowa 2144.

Courtesy of Spook Cave, Iowa.

Spook Cave has a slogan, "Have boats—will travel." The entire trip through the cave is made in aluminum boats powered by silent electric outboard motors. There are 12 boats available for tourist trips, each manned by a guide. The trip starts from a small outdoor lake formed by a dam built to maintain an equal level of water in the cave. The water is about 4 feet deep, and the rocky bottom can be seen as the boat moves through the clear water in the cave.

Open May 1 to November 1, 8:00 A.M. to 5:00 P.M. in spring and fall, and until 6:00 P.M. in summer.

Guided boat ride: 40 minutes.

Rates: adults, $1.50; children, $0.75; group rates available.

On premises: snack bar, gift shop, camping, trailer camp, picnicking, Spook Cave Water Wheel. *Nearby:* all facilities in nearby resort areas.

Nearby attractions: Wonder Cave, Kickapoo Caverns (Wisconsin), Moody's Museum, Mississippi River boat trips, Echo Valley State Park, Brush Creek Canyon State Park, Backbone State Park, Bixby State Park, Sievert Springs Norwegian Museum, Dewey Historical Memorial, Mississippi Wildlife and Fish Refuge, Effigy Mound National Monument, Pike's Peak State Park, Villa Louis (Wisconsin), Museum of Medical Progress (Wisconsin), Yellow River State Forest, Wylusing State Park (Wisconsin), Luther College, resorts, fishing, swimming.

IOWA

WONDER CAVE,
Rural Route 2,
Decorah. U.S. 52
then Iowa 9, about
3 miles northeast of
Decorah. Phone:
319-382-4769.

Courtesy of Wonder Cave, Iowa.

Wonder Cave has many formations, including a huge and perfectly formed stalactite and many pools. In portions the ceilings are 150 feet high. The cave was discovered in 1935, and commercialized in 1936.

Open May 1 to October 1, 8:30 A.M. to 6:00 P.M. daily.

Guided tour: 40 minutes.

Rates: adults, $1.25; children 9 to 15, $0.75; under 9, free; groups of 15 or more, $0.50.

On premises: gift shop, camping, picnicking. *Nearby:* restaurant, snack bar, camping, motels, hotel, cabins, trailer camp, picnicking, go-cart rides, dancing.

Nearby attractions: Spook Cave, Echo Valley State Park, Effigy Mounds National Monument, Mystery Cave (Minnesota), Minnesota Caverns (Minnesota), Bily Clocks, Fort Atkinson, Norwegian-American Historical Museum, Luther College, Niagara Cave (Minnesota), Beaver Creek Valley (Minnesota), world's smallest church.

MINNESOTA

MINNESOTA CAVERNS,
Spring Valley.

Courtesy of Minnesota Caverns, Minnesota.

All information for Minnesota Caverns is the same as information given under Mystery Cave, which is operated under the same ownership. Although the caves are 2 miles apart, the central office is at Mystery Cave. The fees for each cave are separate. Here you are entering the passage called "Fifth Avenue."

Courtesy of Mystery Cave, Minnesota.

MINNESOTA

MYSTERY CAVE, Spring Valley. Off U.S. 16 and 63, about 8 miles southeast of Spring Valley. Phone: Cherry Grove WE7-2418.

Mystery Cave is operated together with Minnesota Caverns 2 miles away. The cave contains this beautiful lake and a river that can be seen on the surface plunging into the side of towering white cliffs before it appears again in Mystery Cave.

Open April 1 to November 1 from 8:00 A.M. to 8:00 P.M.

Guided tour: 1 hour.

Rates: adults, $1.50; children 6 through 12, $0.75; group rates available. (Rates are for Mystery Cave or Minnesota Cave.)

On premises: gift shop, camping, picnicking. *Nearby:* restaurant, snack bar, motels, hotel, cabins.

Nearby attractions: White Water State Park, Niagara Cave, State Fish Hatchery, Pioneer State Park (Iowa), Rochester Medical Center, James Carley State Park, Wonder Cave (Iowa).

Courtesy of Niagara Cave, Minnesota.

MINNESOTA

NIAGARA CAVE, RFD Route 2, Harmony. On U.S. 52 and State 139, about 4 miles southwest of Harmony. Phone: 507-886-5131.

Niagara Cave is known for its mazelike passageways, a stream that meanders the entire distance of the cave, and a 60-foot waterfall. Notice the curious and unique rock formations pictured here. At one point a bridge crosses the stream 60 feet below, while the cavern dome can be seen 70 feet above. Discovered in 1924, commercialized in 1934.

Open all year from 8:00 A.M. to 7:00 P.M. in summer, and from 10:00 A.M. to 4:00 P.M. in winter.

Guided tour: 1 hour.

Rates: adults, $1.50; children, $0.75; group rates: adults, $0.90; children 6 through 12, $0.50; 13 through 18, $0.75.

On premises: snack bar, gift shop, camping, trailer camp, picnicking, baby sitters.

Nearby: motels, hotels.

Nearby attractions: Beaver Creek Valley State Park, Wonder Cave (Iowa), Mystery Cave, Silver Springs Norwegian Museum (Iowa).

Courtesy of John Brown's Cave, Nebraska.

NEBRASKA

JOHN BROWN'S CAVE, Highway 2, Nebraska City.
On State Highway 2 in west part of Nebraska City.
Phone: 402-873-5208.

One of the most important stations of the famous Underground Railroad, John Brown's Cave was actually dug by friends of John Brown. It is not known how many slaves were hidden in the cave, but a great many were transported from the cave across the nearby Missouri River. Pictured is the rear entrance from which slaves used to escape during the night.

Open April to November.

Self-guided tour: no lights necessary, as cave is lighted.

Rates: $0.25 per person.

On premises: restaurant, gift shop, picnicking. *Nearby:* all facilities in Nebraska City.

Nearby attractions: Arbor Lodge State Park, Nebraska State Teachers College, Riverview Park and Marina, Fort Kearney Blockhouse, Steinhart Recreation Park, Waubonsie State Park (Iowa).

NEBRASKA

ROBBER'S CAVE
3243 South 10th,
Lincoln. U.S. 77 and
State Highway 2
south of Lincoln
(in city limits).
Phone:
402-432-7092.

Courtesy of Robber's Cave, Nebraska.

Robber's Cave was once called Pawnee Council Cave. Since the time Jesse James holed up in the cave for 3 days after robbing the Northfield Bank, it has been known by its present name. The cave is formed from Dakota sandstone, not limestone. It has 500 feet of tunnels, some of which are believed to have been enlarged by thieves and robbers. Visitors can cook their meals in an underground fireplace. There are picnic tables in the cave. While most caves are in limestone, this view is typical of sandstone caves, where few formations are found.

Open all year from 10:00 A.M. to 11:00 P.M.

Rates: adults, $0.75; children, $0.25; group rates available.

On premises: gift shop, picnicking. *Nearby:* restaurant, camping, motels, cabins, trailer camp, picnicking.

Nearby attractions: Lincoln (state capital) Zoo, Amusement Park, Home of William Jennings Bryan, Memphis Lake Recreation Grounds, Louisville Lake Recreation Grounds, Blue Stem Recreation Grounds, Wagon Train Recreation Grounds, Blue River Recreation Grounds, Nebraska Wesleyan University, University of Nebraska, Union College.

SOUTH DAKOTA

BETHLEHEM CAVE,
Shrine of the
Nativity, Bethlehem.
3 miles west of U.S.
14, about 20 miles
northwest of Rapid
City. Phone:
605-787-4606.

Courtesy of Bethlehem Cave, South Dakota.

A portion of this cave has been dedicated (the ceremony is pictured here) as a shrine to St. Benedict, the patron saint of cave explorers, by the Benedictine Fathers, who have a monastery on the property. The entrance is on the face of a cliff 270 feet above the floor of Elk Canyon, and provides a spectacular view of the canyon. Formerly known as Old Crystal Cave, it was accessible only by a railway to the bottom of the canyon. Today the grounds and cave are easily reached by car. Features in the cave include dogtooth spar, aragonite crystals, and cave pearls.

Shrine open all year, 8:00 A.M. to 6:30 P.M. Lower cave open June to September, 8:30 A.M. to 5:30 P.M.

Guided tour: 45 minutes.

Rates: no charge for either shrine or cave, and no offerings or collections.

On premises: snack bar, gift shop, picnicking. *Nearby:* all facilities.

Nearby attractions: Nameless Cave, Sitting Bull Crystal Cave, Stage Barn Crystal Cave, Thunder Head Falls, Wild Cat Cave, Wonderland Cave, Jewel Cave National Monument, Rushmore Cave, Wind Cave National Park, Mount Rushmore National Memorial, Reptile Gardens, Custer State Park, Sylvan Lake, Castle Creek State Park, Deerfield Lake, Black Fox Recreation Area, Deadwood, Dinosaur Park, South Dakota State School of Mines and Museum, Petrified Forest, Crazy Horse Monument, Bear Butte State Park, gold and lead mines.

124

Courtesy of Jewel Cave National Monument, South Dakota.
Photo by National Park Service.

SOUTH DAKOTA

JEWEL CAVE NATIONAL MONUMENT, c/o Wind Cave National Park, Hot Springs. U.S. 16, about 14 miles west of Custer (administered by, but not in, Wind Cave National Park). Phone: Wind Cave, Hot Springs, S.D. 2301.

The walls of many of the underground chambers of Jewel Cave are lined with a solid coating of dogtooth calcite crystals, as is shown here. These sparkle like jewels in the light. Because of these colorful formations, the cave and a protective surface area of 1,275 acres were set aside as a National Monument in 1908. Originally believed to be a rather small cave, 13½ miles have been mapped since 1959. A development program has been begun by the National Park Service to provide access and new tour routes in the newly discovered portions of the cave, which include some fine wet formations, unusual in Black Hills caves. The new development will not be open to the public until late 1967 or 1968.

Open June 1 to Labor Day, 8:00 A.M. to 5:00 P.M.

Guided tour: 1 hour and 15 minutes. Tour not recommended for those in poor physical condition. Old clothes and stout walking shoes should be worn. Development has been kept to a minimum, and rangers supply gasoline lanterns for lighting.

Rates: adults, $0.50; children under 16, free, but must be accompanied by adults responsible for their safety and conduct. Children under 5 not permitted in cave.

On premises: picnicking. *Nearby:* all facilities in Custer, 14 miles from cave.

Nearby attractions: Bethlehem Cave, Nameless Cave, Sitting Bull Crystal Caverns,

125

Stage Barn Crystal Cave, Thunder Head Falls, Wild Cat Cave, Wonderland Cave, Rushmore Cave, Mount Rushmore National Memorial, Custer State Park, Sylvan Lake, Deerfield Lake, Black Fox Recreation Area, Dinosaur Park, South Dakota State School of Mines and Museum, Reptile Gardens, Crazy Horse Monument, Cold Brook Reservoir, Angostura Recreation Area, Angostura Reservoir and Dam, Gull Hill Roadside Park.

SOUTH DAKOTA

NAMELESS CAVE, R.R. 1, Box 127A, Rapid City. State Highway 40, about 3½ miles west of Rapid City. Phone: 434-0542.

Although this cave was discovered in 1880, it was not until 1934 that it was lighted and opened to the public. The entrance, located at the bottom of a canyon, permits access to a series of rooms with examples of dogtooth spar, boxwork, and popcorn. Entire rooms are coated with tiny crystals, some redissolved by later solution.

Open June through Labor Day from 6:30 A.M. to 10:00 P.M.

Guided tour: 45 minutes.

Rates: adults, $1.00; children, $0.35.

On premises: gift shop. *Nearby:* restaurant, camping, motel, hotel, cabins, trailer camp, picnicking, baby sitters.

Nearby attractions: Wild Cat Cave, Thunder Head Falls, Bethlehem Cave, Sitting Bull Crystal Cave, Stage Barn Crystal Cave, Wonderland Cave, Jewel Cave National Monument, Rushmore Cave, Wind Cave National Monument, Mount Rushmore National Memorial, Custer State Park, Sylvan Lake, Castle Creek State Park, Deerfield Lake, Black Fox Recreation Area, Deadwood, Dinosaur Park, South Dakota State School of Mines and Museum, Crazy Horse Monument, gold and lead mines.

SOUTH DAKOTA

RUSHMORE CAVE,
Keystone. Off U.S.
16A. Phone:
605-255-4467.

Courtesy of Rushmore Cave, South Dakota.

Rushmore Cave, unlike most of the caves in the area, contains these beautiful stalactites and stalagmites. There are fewer crystals and dogtooth spar than you would ordinarily expect.

Open May 1 through October 31. June, July, and August, open 24 hours a day. Other times, 7:00 A.M. to 7:00 P.M.

Guided tour: 45 minutes to 1 hour.

Rates: adults, $1.25; children 7 through 12, $0.50. Groups: adults, $0.75; children, $0.50.

On premises: snack bar, gift shop. *Nearby:* restaurant, camping, motels, hotels, cabins, trailer camp, picnicking.

Nearby attractions: Custer State Park, Reptile Gardens, Mount Rushmore Memorial, Deadwood, Bethlehem Cave, Wonderland Cave, Stage Barn Crystal Cave, Sitting Bull Crystal Caverns, Nameless Cave, Thunder Head Falls, Jewel Cave National Monument, Wind Cave National Park.

Courtesy of Sitting Bull Crystal Caverns, South Dakota.

SOUTH DAKOTA

SITTING BULL CRYSTAL CAVERNS, Box 1649, Rapid
City. 9 miles south of Rapid City on U.S. 16 (Mount
Rushmore Road). Phone: 605-342-2777.

Sitting Bull Crystal Caverns is famous for its dogtooth spar crystals—a rarity in caves. In places the ceilings are covered with these large crystals. There are 3 sections that form the cave; the first drops 156 feet, and contains the dogtooth spar; next is Diamond Lake, 1,256 feet beneath the mountain, and filled with schools of living fish. It also contains a petrified fish crevice. The third section is 100 feet lower. The cave was discovered in 1876 and commercialized in 1930. Pictured is the cave entrance.

Open March to December, daily from 6:00 A.M. to 8:00 P.M.
Guided tour: 30 minutes.
Rates: adults, $1.00; children, $0.50; group rates available.
On premises: picnicking. *Nearby:* restaurants, snack bar, gift shop, camping, motels, hotels, cabins, trailer camp.
Nearby attractions: Bethlehem Cave, Nameless Cave, Stage Barn Crystal Cave, Thunder Head Falls, Wild Cat Cave, Wonderland Cave, Jewel Cave National Monument, Rushmore Cave, Wind Cave National Monument, Mount Rushmore National Memorial, Custer State Park, Sylvan Lake, Castle Creek State Park, Reptile Gardens, Deerfield Lake, Black Fox Recreation Area, Deadwood, Dinosaur Park, South Dakota State School of Mines and Museum, Petrified Forest, Crazy Horse Monument, Bear Butte State Park, gold and lead mines.

Courtesy of Stage Barn Crystal Cave, South Dakota.

SOUTH DAKOTA

STAGE BARN CRYSTAL CAVE, Box 94, Piedmont.
11 miles north of Rapid City and 2 miles west of Interstate 90, 14, and 79. Phone: None.

Stage Barn Crystal Cave is in Stage Barn Canyon, originally part of the Deadwood Stage route from Deadwood to Sidney, Nebraska. Remains of an old mining railroad can be seen in the canyon. The cave is well decorated. It was discovered in 1924 and commercialized in 1935. The picture shows an interesting ridge of white stalagmites and flowstone formed from the drippings from the small stalactites above.
Open April 1 to October 16, 6:00 A.M. to 9:00 P.M. daily.
Guided tour: 45 to 60 minutes.
Rates: adults, $1.20; children 6 to 12 years, $0.60; under 6, free; groups, half price.
On premises: no facilities. *Nearby:* all facilities available.
Nearby attractions: Bethlehem Cave, Nameless Cave, Sitting Bull Crystal Caverns, Thunder Head Falls, Wild Cat Cave, Wonderland Cave, Jewel Cave National Monument, Rushmore Cave, Wind Cave National Park, Mount Rushmore National Memorial, Custer State Park, Sylvan Lake, Deerfield Lake, Reptile Gardens, Deadwood, Dinosaur Park, South Dakota State School of Mines and Museum, Petrified Forest, Crazy Horse Monument, Bear Butte State Park, gold mines.

SOUTH DAKOTA

THUNDER HEAD FALLS, Route 1, Box 117C, Rapid City. State Highway 40 west of Rapid City. Phone: 605-343-0707.

Courtesy of Thunder Head Falls, South Dakota.

Thunder Head Falls is actually not a cave. It is the remnant of a gold-mining operation, one tunnel of which here reveals a waterfall 2 blocks within the mountain. By removing tons of boulders, building a 600-foot walkway, and constructing 6 bridges, the 9-cubic-foot-per-second waterfall was made accessible to the public. It was opened in 1950.

Open May through September, dawn to dusk.

Tour: 30 minutes.

Rates: adults, $0.85; children, $0.35.

On premises: no facilities. *Nearby:* all facilities.

Nearby attractions: Bethlehem Cave, Nameless Cave, Sitting Bull Crystal Caverns, Stage Barn Crystal Cave, Wild Cat Cave, Wonderland Cave, Jewel Cave National Monument, Rushmore Cave, Wind Cave National Park, Mount Rushmore National Memorial, Custer State Park, Sylvan Lake, Castle Creek State Park, Deerfield Lake, Black Fox Recreation Area, Reptile Gardens, Deadwood, Dinosaur Park, South Dakota School of Mines and Museum, Petrified Forest, Crazy Horse Monument, Bear Butte State Park, gold and lead mines.

Courtesy of Wild Cat Cave, South Dakota.

SOUTH DAKOTA

WILD CAT CAVE, Rural Route 1, Rapid City. Off
State Route 40 between Rapid City and Silver City.

Wild Cat Cave has been known to cave explorers for over 50 years. It is large, well decorated, and even today a portion of the cave has not been explored. The formation shown is known as the "Alligator."
Open all year from 6:00 A.M. to dusk.
Guided tour: 1 hour.
Rates: adults, $1.10; children, $0.45.
On premises: snack bar, gift shop, picnicking. *Nearby:* camping, motels, hotels, trailer camp, baby sitters.
Nearby attractions: Bethlehem Cave, Nameless Cave, Sitting Bull Crystal Caverns, Stage Barn Crystal Cave, Thunder Head Falls, Wonderland Cave, Jewel Cave National Monument, Rushmore Cave, Wind Cave National Park, Mount Rushmore National Memorial, Custer State Park, Sylvan Lake, Castle Creek State Park, Deerfield Lake, Reptile Gardens, Black Fox Recreation Area, Deadwood, Dinosaur Park, South Dakota State School of Mines and Museum, Petrified Forest, Crazy Horse Monument, Bear Butte State Park, gold and lead mines.

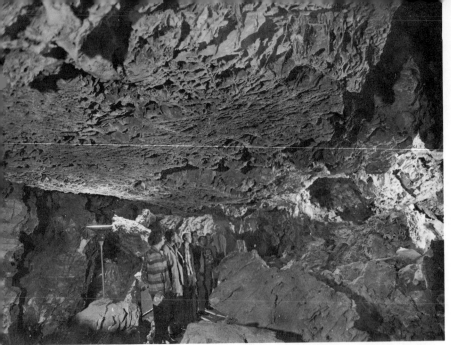

Courtesy of Wind Cave National Park, South Dakota. National Park Service Photo.

SOUTH DAKOTA

WIND CAVE NATIONAL PARK, Hot Springs. U.S. 385 and S.D. 87. Phone: WC2301.

The currents of air that blow in and out of Wind Cave suggested the park's name. The strange phenomenon is believed to be caused by changes in atmospheric pressure. Bison roam over the park's 44 square miles of rolling, wooded, and plains country. Elk, pronghorn, and other wildlife also live in this part of the Black Hills. The cave was discovered in 1881, and in 1892 it was opened for visitors. In January, 1903, President Theodore Roosevelt signed a bill establishing Wind Cave National Park. The cave itself is noted for the unusual "boxwork," shown here on the roof of the cave, caused by water carrying calcium carbonate that evaporates along the many cracks and fractures. Displays of unusual "frostwork," "popcorn," and dog-tooth spar are found. The tour covers 1¼ miles of 4½ miles of explored passageway. *Open* April 1 to October 31 daily from 8:00 A.M. to 5:00 P.M., depending on help. *Guided tour:* 1 and 1½ hours.

Rates: adults, $0.75; children under 16, free. No group rate.

On premises: snack bar, gift shop, camping, picnicking, nature trail, museum exhibits, campfire talks. *Nearby:* restaurant, motels, hotels, cabins, trailer camp.

Nearby attractions: Mount Rushmore National Memorial, Custer State Park, Sylvan Lake, Deerfield Lake, Black Fox Recreation Area, Dinosaur Park, South Dakota State School of Mines and Museum, Crazy Horse Monument, Reptile Gardens, Cold Brook Reservoir, Angostura Recreation Area, Angostura Reservoir and Dam, Gull Hill Roadside Park, Bethlehem Cave, Nameless Cave, Sitting Bull Crystal Caverns, Stage Barn Crystal Cave, Thunder Head Falls, Wild Cat Cave, Wonderland Cave, Jewel Cave National Monument, Rushmore Cave.

Courtesy of Wonderland Cave, South Dakota.

SOUTH DAKOTA

WONDERLAND CAVE, Box 83, Nemo. Off Interstate 90 and State 14 between Rapid City and Sturgis, or off State Route 385 via Nemo. Phone: 605-578-1728.

Wonderland Cave is developed on 2 levels, with miles of passageways. The formation pictured is known as "Icicle Fence," and is the pride of Wonderland Cave. It is a row of stalactites 40 feet long. The cave was discovered in 1929 and commercialized in 1930.

Open May 1 through October 31, 24 hours daily.

Guided tour: 40 minutes.

Rates: adults, $1.00; children, $0.60; 6 and under, free.

On premises: snack bar, gift shop, picnicking. *Nearby:* restaurants, camping, motels, hotels, cabins, trailer camp.

Nearby attractions: Mount Rushmore National Memorial, Custer State Park, Sylvan Lake, Castle Creek State Park, Deerfield Lake, Black Fox Recreation Area, Deadwood, Dinosaur Park, South Dakota State School of Mines and Museum, Petrified Forest, Reptile Gardens, Crazy Horse Monument, Bear Butte State Park, Bethlehem Cave, Nameless Cave, Sitting Bull Crystal Caverns, Stage Barn Crystal Cave, Thunder Head Falls, Wild Cat Cave, Christ on the Mountain, Black Hills Passion Play, Adams Memorial Museum, Terry Peak Chair Lift, gold mines.

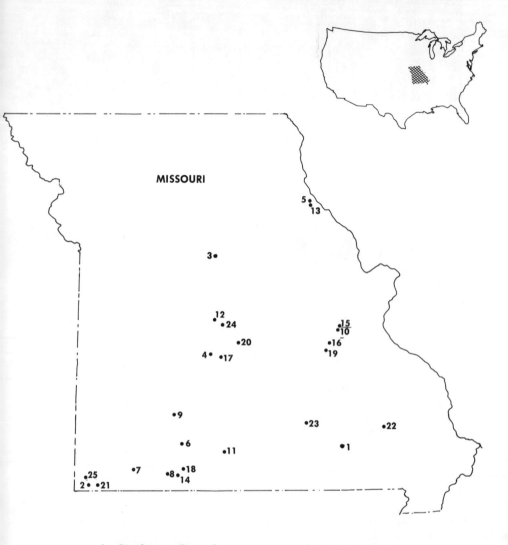

MISSOURI

1. Big Spring Onyx Caverns
2. Bluff Dwellers Cave
3. Boone Cave
4. Bridal Cave
5. Cameron Cave
6. Civil War Cave
7. Crystal Caverns
8. Fairy Cave
9. Fantastic Caverns
10. Fisher's Cave
11. Honey Branch Cave
12. Jacob's Cave
13. Mark Twain Cave

14. Marvel Cave
15. Meramec Caverns
16. Missouri Caverns
17. Mystic River Cave
18. Old Spanish Cave
19. Onondaga Cave
20. Ozark Caverns
21. Ozark Wonder Cave
22. Rebel Cave
23. Round Spring Cavern
24. Stark Caverns
25. Truitt's Cave

6. MISSOURI REGION

There are more tourist caves in the state of Missouri than in any other state. The Ozark Plateau and Ozark and Boston Mountain regions of the state have long been a vacation area. The beautiful countryside and natural attractions have brought visitors from all over the country. It could well be said that Missouri is the cave state of the country. Most of the examples of limestone cave formations are found in the caves open to the public, and a great variety of cave types can be seen. Some of the largest springs in the United States drain the limestone country, and underground streams within the caves are not uncommon. Creatures adapted to the complete darkness of caves, such as white blind salamanders and crayfish are more profuse in this region than most others. Historical evidences of Indian, Spanish, and colonial occupancy are also found.

Courtesy of Big Spring Onyx Caverns, Missouri.

MISSOURI

BIG SPRING ONYX CAVERNS, Box 151, Van Buren.
1 mile west of Van Buren on U.S. 60.

Formerly known as Cave Springs Onyx Caverns, Big Spring Onyx Caverns was used as a hiding-place station on the Underground Railroad by means of which slaves were transported to freedom. It was also used for three weeks as a hideout by Jesse James and his henchmen after they committed the famous Gad's Hill Train Robbery. The cave is operated as a nonprofit organization, and the park, owned by the cave, is a wildlife sanctuary. A free zoo is maintained, and fishing at no cost and without license is permitted. Pictured here is the entrance to Section 7, which is filled with various colored onyx formations.

Open all year, 24 hours a day.

Self-guided tour through 10 lighted rooms.

Rates: adults, $0.75 plus $0.25 for special lights, which are also provided. Children, $0.25 plus $0.10 for special lights. (These rates are on a membership basis, and entitle purchasers to use of facilities for three years.)

On premises: snack bar, gift shop, free camping, cabins, picnicking, swimming, zoo, wildlife sanctuary, fishing. *Nearby:* motels, hotel, swimming, fishing, games.

Nearby attractions: Clark National Forest, Deer Run Wildlife Area, Sam Baker State Park, Bozarth Tract State Forest, Clearwater Lake, Miller Community Lake, New National Ozark Rivers Scenic Park, Wappapello Reservoir, Lake Wappapello State Park.

MISSOURI

BLUFF DWELLERS CAVE,
Route 2, Box 229,
Noel. State Highway
59, about 2 miles
south of Noel.
Phone:
417-475-3666.

Courtesy of Bluff Dwellers Cave, Missouri.

Bluff Dwellers Cave derives its name from the human bones and stone implements found under the exit cliff when the cave was being developed commercially
in 1927. These artifacts are on display at the cave entrance. On the road approaching the cave, huge overhanging cliffs can be seen that also served as shelters for
occupants predating the white man. Shown are the cave stalactite curtains that pro-
duce a range of tones when tapped by the guides.

Open all year, 8:00 A.M. to 6:00 P.M.
Guided tour: 45 minutes.
Rates: adults, $1.00; children 10 to 12, $0.50; from 6 to 9, $0.25; under 6, free.
Group rates for 16 or more, $0.50.
On premises: gift shop, mineral museum, picnicking. *Nearby:* restaurant, snack bar,
camping, motels, hotels, cabins, trailer camp.
Nearby attractions: "Christmas City of Noel," "Prize Drive of the Ozarks," Shadow
Lake, George Washington Carver National Monument, Lake of the Cherokees
(Oklahoma), Honey Creek Recreational Area (Oklahoma), Roaring River State
Park, Truitt's Cave, Ozark Wonder Cave, Civil War Cave (Arkansas), Old Spanish
Treasure Cave (Arkansas), Onyx Cave (Arkansas), Wonderland Cave (Arkansas),
Crystal Caverns, Ozark National Forest, Neosho Spring, lead mines, zinc mines.

137

Courtesy of Boone Cave, Missouri.

MISSOURI

BOONE CAVE, Rocheport. 1½ miles south of U.S. 70, Rocheport exit on State BB. Phone: 314-OX-2285.

Boone Cave has a history of occupancy dating to the Ice Age. Bones of the woolly mammoth, musk ox, and fragments of extinct bison have been found in the cave. In 1812, it was used as a storehouse for gunpowder for the forts along the Missouri River. During the Civil War it sheltered guerrilla fighters and bands of "bushwackers" from both sides. Later on, it became a retreat of river pirates who raided steamboats that stopped at the Rocheport dock. Today the cave is open to the public, and is partly lighted with flaring torches to recall the days when the cave sheltered earlier men, both good and bad. Shown is the entrance to the cave.

Open April through November, 8:00 A.M. to 5:00 P.M.

Guided tour: 1 hour.

Rates: adults, $1.25; children 6 to 12, $0.60; under 6, free.

On premises: gift shop, camping, picnicking. *Nearby:* restaurant, motel, trailer camp. *Nearby attractions:* Arrow Rock, Thespian Hall, Van Meter State Park, Chance Gardens, University of Missouri at Columbia.

MISSOURI

BRIDAL CAVE,
Camdenton.
Missouri Highway 5,
about 3½ miles north
of Camdenton.
Phone:
314-346-2676.

Courtesy of Bridal Cave, Missouri.

Bridal Cave is on the shores of Lake of the Ozarks, and can be reached by boat as well as by road. Originally named Bridal Cave from the marriage of the Osage Indian Princess Irona to the Indian brave Prince Buffalo, it has since been the scene of hundreds of weddings, such as this one, in the "Bridal Chapel" within the cave. It is highly decorated, and its size is still undetermined because it has been explored only to a subterranean lake.

Open all year, from 8:00 A.M. to sundown.

Guided tour: 30 minutes.

Rates: adults, $1.50; children 6 through 11, $0.75; under 6, free. Group rates available.

On premises: gift shop. *Nearby:* all facilities on and near the Lake of the Ozarks, including 400 resorts.

Nearby attractions: Lake of the Ozarks resort area, Jacobs Cave, Stark Caverns, Ozark Caverns, Mystic River Cave, Lake of the Ozarks State Park, Bennett Springs State Park, Osage Beach, Bagnell Dam, Ha Ha Tonka Castle.

CAMERON CAVE, Box 26, Hannibal. Off U.S. 61, about 2 miles south of Hannibal on State Highway 79. Phone: 314-221-1656.

Cameron Cave is similar to Mark Twain Cave, and has 4 miles of passageway. However, the tour of ½ mile of cave is made with lanterns instead of electric lights, giving the visitor an eerie view of the cave, which has the same ownership as nearby Mark Twain Cave.

Open June 1 to October 1, 8:00 A.M. to 5:00 P.M. daily.

Guided tour: 45 minutes. Lanterns supplied.

Rates: $1.00; children 5 through 11, $0.50.

On premises: no facilities. *Nearby:* all facilities at Mark Twain Cave or in Hannibal.

Nearby attractions: Mark Twain Cave, Mark Twain's Boyhood Home, Mark Twain Statue, Mark Twain Museum, and other Mark Twain buildings, Cardiff Hill and Lighthouse, Lover's Leap, Dam 2 at Saverton, Old Historic Packet Boat, Mark Twain State Park, riverboat trips.

Courtesy of Civil War Cave, Missouri.

MISSOURI

CIVIL WAR CAVE, Route 2, Ozark. 4 miles east of
U.S. 65, just north of Ozark. Phone: 417-485-2396.

Boasting a huge entrance, Civil War Cave, formerly Smallin Cave, was used
as a munitions warehouse by General Lyon's forces at the bloody battle of Wilson's
Creek on August 9, 1861. The cave was used as a shelter by the Osage Indians. Dis-
covered in 1818, commercialized in 1962. There are no steps in the cave.
Open May through September daily from 7:00 A.M. to 7:00 P.M.
Guided tour: 30 minutes.
Rates: adults, $1.10; children 6 to 12, $0.50; under 6, free.
On premises: gift shop, picnicking, Abraham Lincoln's Funeral Coach, Civil War
Museum, Old Time Log Fort. *Nearby:* restaurant, snack bar, motels, hotels.
Nearby attractions: Old Spanish Cave, Crystal Cave, Fantastic Caverns, Silver Dol-
lar City, Riverside Inn, Fairy Cave, Marvel Cave, Drury College, Wilson's Creek
Battlefield, Springfield National Cemetery, Table Rock Reservoir, Southwest Missouri
State Teachers College.

CRYSTAL CAVERNS, Cassville. On State Business Route 37, about ½ mile north of the Cassville business district. No phone.

There is a legend that many years ago an Indian maiden who was being pursued dived from the high bluff near Crystal Caverns and swam underwater, emerging in Crystal Caverns, and thereby outwitting her pursuers. In any event, the surrounding area and indeed the cave itself have produced hundreds of Indian artifacts—especially bows and arrows and arrowheads.

Open all year, dawn to dusk.

Guided tour: 30 minutes.

Rates: adults, $0.85; children, $0.85; under 6, free.

On premises: picnicking, baby sitters. *Nearby:* all facilities in Cassville and surrounding recreational area.

Nearby attractions: Roaring River State Park, Deer Park, Table Rock Lake, Ozark Frontier Trails, Ozark Wonder Cave, Fairy Cave, Marvel Cave, Old Spanish Cave, Civil War Cave, Onyx Cave (Arkansas), Eagle Rock State Park, Bluff Dwellers Cave, Truitt's Cave, horseback riding, boating, fishing, resort area.

MISSOURI

FAIRY CAVE,
Reed's Spring. On
State Highway 13,
south of Reed's
Spring. Phone:
417-272-3616.

Courtesy of Fairy Cave, Missouri.
Photo by Walker—Missouri Commerce.

A highly decorated cave, Fairy Cave was first explored by Truman S. Powell in 1896, 13 years after its discovery. Powell was the famous shepherd in Harold Bell Wright's novel *The Shepherd of the Hills*. The Powell family still runs the cave. Because the cave developed in a vertical fissure, tourists use a series of stairways hidden among the huge formations. A beautiful wall of flowstone can be seen in the photograph.

Open all year, 8:00 A.M. to 6:00 P.M. daily.

Guided tour: 35 to 40 minutes.

Rates: adults, $1.50; children, $0.50; groups of 10 or more, $0.50 each.

On premises: 1,500-acre preserve, picnicking, horseback riding. *Nearby:* restaurant, snack bar, gift shop, camping, motels, trailer camp.

Nearby attractions: Marvel Cave, Silver Dollar City, Old Spanish Cave, Crystal Caverns, Civil War Cave, Onyx Cave (Arkansas).

MISSOURI

FANTASTIC CAVERNS, Route 11, Box 1933, Springfield. 4 miles northwest of Springfield on State Highway 13. Phone: 417-365-4010.

The entire tour of Fantastic Caverns is made over a 1-mile trail by a jeep towing an open trailer. A stage show is held on Saturdays at 8:00 P.M. in the ' auditorium in the cave.

Open all year, 8:00 A.M. to dusk.

Guided tour by jeep: 30 minutes.

Rates: adults, $1.50; children, $0.75. Group rates available.

On premises: snack bar, gift shop, camping, picnicking, horseback riding. *Nearby:* restaurant, camping, motels, trailer camp.

Nearby attractions: Crystal Cave, Civil War Cave, Wilson's Creek Battlefield, Springfield, Old Spanish Cave, Marvel Cave, Drury College, Missouri State Teachers College.

FISHER'S CAVE, Meramec State Park, Sullivan. On State Highway 155, just south of U.S. 66 at Sullivan. Phone: 314-468-6072.

Meramec State Park contains over 20 caves, of which Fisher's Cave is the most interesting. It is the only cave in the park in which guided tours are conducted. Visitors are furnished with lamps for the tour.

Open May through October, 9:00 A.M. to 5:00 P.M.

Guided tour: 1 hour. Lanterns furnished.

Rates: Adults, $0.90; children, $0.60; under 12, free.

On premises: snack bar, gift shop, camping, lodge, cabins, trailer camp, picnicking, swimming, playground, sports fields, horseback riding, nature museum, naturalist in summer. *Nearby:* restaurant, motels, hotel, cabins.

Nearby attractions: Missouri Caverns, Onondaga Cave, Washington State Park, Meramec Caverns.

MISSOURI

HONEY BRANCH CAVE,
Elkhead. 1 mile
south of State
Highway 14,
west of Ava.
Phone:
417-683-0269.

Courtesy of Honey Branch Cave, Missouri.

Discovered by Indians in 1835, Honey Branch Cave was commercialized in 1956. The cave operates a museum and an Old Log House. It is level and there are no steps.

Open all year, 8:00 A.M. to 5:00 P.M.

Guided tour: 45 minutes.

Rates: adults, $1.00; children, $0.50; groups of 20 or more, half price.

On premises: snack bar, gift shop, camping, cabins, trailer camp. *Nearby:* hotel, motels.

Nearby attractions: Civil War Cave, Crystal Cave, Table Rock, Mark Twain National Forest.

145

Courtesy of Jacob's Cave, Missouri.

MISSOURI

JACOB'S CAVE,
Versailles. 2 miles
off State Highway 5,
on T T Road
about 6 miles south
of Versailles. Phone:
314-378-4374.

Jacob's Cave, at the northern tip of Lake of the Ozarks, was discovered by a lead and zinc miner in 1875. Geologists and paleontologists from the Missouri State Capital Museum and the Walker Museum of Paleontology in Chicago have discovered and studied fossil teeth, skulls, and skeletal parts of peccaries and other prehistoric animals in the cave. Since there are no steps in the cave, baby carriages and wheelchairs can be used. The formation in the photograph is known as the "Elephant's Head."

Open all year, 10 hours daily.

Guided tour: 35 minutes.

Rates: adults, $1.00; children, $0.50. Group rates available.

On premises: gift shop, snack bar, camping, picnicking. *Nearby:* restaurant, motels, hotels, cabins, resorts.

Nearby attractions: Lake of the Ozarks, many tourist and summer resorts, geographical center of the U.S., Lake of the Ozarks State Park, Stark Caverns, Ozark Caverns, Bridal Cave, Bagnell Dam, Rebel Cave, Ha Ha Tonka Castle.

Courtesy of Mark Twain Cave, Missouri.

MISSOURI

MARK TWAIN CAVE, P.O. Box 26, Hannibal. 2 miles south of Hannibal on State Route 79. New highway opens spring, 1966.

Mark Twain Cave is well known to lovers of Samuel Clemens, as it was referred to and described in many of his writings. The best description of the cave appears in Twain's *The Adventures of Tom Sawyer,* as it was in this cave that Becky Thatcher and Tom Sawyer were lost. The cave had a great influence on Mark Twain's life, and many of the incidents he described were related to his personal experiences. At one time the cave was known as McDowell's Cave for a Dr. McDowell of St. Louis who placed a child's body there as a tourist attraction, thinking it would petrify. In the photograph are two youngsters contemplating how Tom Sawyer must have felt when he was lost in the cave with Becky Thatcher. This is the spot at which they were reputed to have been found.

Open all year from 8:00 A.M. to 5:00 P.M. in winter, and 8:00 A.M. to 8:00 P.M. in summer.

Guided tour: 30 to 45 minutes.

Rates: adults, $1.00; children, $0.50; group rates for 20 or more, $0.50 each.

On premises: snack bar, gift shop, picnicking. *Nearby:* all facilities in Hannibal.

Nearby attractions: Mark Twain's Boyhood Home, Mark Twain Statue, Mark Twain Museum and other Mark Twain buildings, Cardiff Hill and Lighthouse, Lover's Leap, Dam 2 at Saverton, Old Historic Packet Boat, riverboat trips, Mark Twain State Park, Cameron Cave, Becky Thatcher House, Tom Sawyer and Huck Finn Statue.

Courtesy of Marvel Cave, Missouri.

MISSOURI

MARVEL CAVE,
Branson. State
Highway 76 west of
Branson. Phone:
417-334-2156.

Marvel Cave has 3 features of major importance. The first is the unusual entranceway through the ceiling of a breathtaking room 20 stories high. At the bottom of this room, an old dance floor looks like a postage stamp to the entering visitors. The room is so large that this balloon, manned by the famous balloonist Piccard, was set free in it. The second is the Marvel Cave waterfall 500 feet beneath the surface. The third is a modern, 3-car cable train that brings all visitors out of the cave without the necessity of going back by way of the 20-story room. Over 12 miles of passageway are known in this highly decorated cave. The owners operate Silver Dollar City on the cave property. This is a complete mining town of 1880 that has 3 thoroughfares and a steam railroad.

Open March through December from 8:00 A.M.

Guided tour: 1¼ hours.

Rates: adults, $1.75; children, $0.75.

On premises: Silver Dollar City, restaurant, snack bar, gift shop. *Nearby:* all facilities.

Nearby attractions: Fairy Cave, Old Spanish Cave, Crystal Caverns, Civil War Cave, Onyx Cave (Arkansas), Bull Shoals Cave (Arkansas), resort areas.

Courtesy of Meramec Caverns, Missouri.

MISSOURI

MERAMEC CAVERNS, Stanton. On U.S. 66-44, south-west of Stanton. Phone: 314-468-4156.

Meramec Caverns is highly decorated and has 26 miles of explored passage. The cave, known since 1716, has a long history of mining operations, gunpowder manufacturing, and has been used as a gangster hangout. Jesse James used this cave, as well as others, as a hideout. "Loot Rock," the room seen in the photograph, contains lifelike figures of some of the James gang, since relics of the gang were found there. The cave contains a river and several mirror-like lakes.

Open all year, 8:00 A.M. to dusk.
Guided tour: 1¼ hours.
Rates: adults, $2.00; children, $1.00 (6 through 12).
On premises: restaurant, snack bar, gift shop, camping, motel, picnicking. *Nearby:* hotels, cabins, trailer camp.
Nearby attractions: Missouri Caverns, Onondaga Cave, Washington State Park, Meramec State Park, Austin's Tomb, Meramec Spring, University of Missouri School of Mines, Huzzah State Forest.

149

MISSOURI

MISSOURI CAVERNS, Leasburg. Off U.S. 66, Interstate 44. Phone: 314-245-3515.

Missouri Caverns, formerly known as Cathedral Cave, is owned by Onondaga Cave, and is operated on a scheduled basis solely for educational tours from schools, universities, and so on. For information, consult Mr. Lyman Riley at the above address.

MYSTIC RIVER CAVE, Camdenton. U.S. 54 to Route K. Phone: 314-DI6-2380.

Mystic River Cave contains a natural bridge, rimstone pools, and a huge stalagmite. On the property are seven other caves, including Counterfeiters', Robbers', and Bear Caves.

Open May to October, 9:00 A.M. to 6:00 P.M. daily.

Guided tour: 30 minutes.

Rates: $0.50 per person.

On premises: restaurant, camping, lodge, cabins, picnicking, fishing, swimming, Ha Ha Tonka Castle, playground, horseback riding, trails.

Nearby attractions: Jacob's Cave, Stark Caverns, Ozark Caverns, Bridal Cave, Lake of the Ozarks resort area, Lake of the Ozarks State Park, Bennett Springs State Park, Osage Beach, Bagnell Dam.

OLD SPANISH CAVE, Reeds Spring. On U.S. 65 about 3 miles north of Reeds Spring Junction (35 miles south of Springfield). Phone: 417-272-3346.

An old Spanish map found in 1885 showed this cave under an overhanging cliff. The map stated that the Spaniards had visited the cave in 1830 and that 3 of their group died and were left in the cave. It also said that silver was mined there and that a subchamber had a rich vein of silver remaining. With the aid of the map, the cave was located, and the entrance was found to be sealed. The first men to enter the cave after digging out the entrance found 3 skeletons covered with a blanket, further proving the authenticity of the map. Crucibles and other evidences of mining were found, but to this day no one has ever discovered the room supposedly containing the silver. The cave was finally commercialized in 1950.

Open all year, 8:00 A.M. to 5:00 P.M.

Guided tour: 45 minutes.

Rates: adults, $1.50; children under 12, free. Groups of 10 or more, $1.00 each.

On premises: gift shop, camping, picnicking. *Nearby:* restaurant, snack bar, motels, hotels, cabins, trailer camp, baby sitters.

Nearby attractions: Fairy Cave, Marvel Cave, Crystal Caverns, Civil War Cave, White River, Silver Dollar City, Onyx Cave (Arkansas), resorts.

MISSOURI

ONONDAGA CAVE,
Leasburg. Off U.S.
66, Interstate 44.
Phone:
314-245-3515.

Courtesy of Onondaga Cave, Missouri.
Photo by Walker—Missouri Commerce.

Onondaga Cave was discovered in 1798 by Daniel Boone, who helped settle the land to the north of the cave. In 1904, the cave was opened to the public to attract visitors from the St. Louis World's Fair. Onondaga is a colorful cave with massive formations, and the "Big Room" is over 2,900 feet in length, 110 feet high, and 321 feet wide. It is famous for its "Lily Pad Room"—rimstone pools with calcite formations in the shape of lily pads on the surface of mirror-like waters. Lost River parallels the walks throughout the cave, and adds to its beauty. Pictured is the "Queen's Canopy" room, one of the largest in any cave.
Open every day all year.
Guided tour: 1 hour and 20 minutes.
Rates: adults, $2.00; children, $1.00.
On premises: restaurant, snack bar, gift shop, camping, picnicking, boating. *Nearby:* motels, hotel, cabins.
Nearby attractions: Huzzah State Forest, Meramec Caverns, Meramec Springs, Meramec State Park, Fisher Cave, Missouri Caverns, Washington State Park, Austin's Tomb, University of Missouri School of Mines.

MISSOURI

OZARK CAVERNS, Osage Beach. State Road A off U.S. 54, about 4 miles south of Osage Beach or 4 miles east of Camdenton.

Ozark Caverns features a special excursion tour that operates twice daily and combines a speedboat ride, a wagon ride, and a tour of the cave. The cave was discovered in 1840 and commercialized in 1952.

Open all year, 8:00 A.M. until sundown daily.

Guided tour: 45 minutes.

Rates (cave only): adults, $1.50; children, $0.75; school groups, $0.50; other groups, $0.75.

On premises: gift shop, picnicking. *Nearby:* resort areas with all facilities.

Nearby attractions: Lake of the Ozarks resort area, Jacob's Cave, Stark Caverns, Bridal Cave, Mystic River Cave, Lake of the Ozarks State Park, Bennett Springs State Park, Osage Beach, Bagnell Dam, Ha Ha Tonka Castle.

MISSOURI

OZARK WONDER CAVE, Route 2, Noel. 4 miles north of Noel and ½ mile east of State Route 59 at Elk Springs. Phone: 417-475-3579.

Courtesy of Ozark Wonder Cave, Missouri.

Ozark Wonder Cave was widely used during the Civil War as an ammunition dump and for other purposes. It has also been a source of many artifacts. Dr. Mark Harrington headed an expedition there for the Museum of the American Indian, Heye Foundation. Many skeletons were found, together with bits of pottery, arrowheads, stone implements, bone tools, wooden needles, and so on. The cave contains 7 rooms, and was discovered in 1862. It was commercialized in 1916. Called "The Columns," this picture shows a fine example of how an entire wall can be built up from a joining of stalactites and stalagmites that are close together.

Open all year, 8:00 A.M. to 8:00 P.M.

Rates: adults, $1.00; children, $0.50; groups, $0.50 each.

On premises: gift shop, resort operated by cave owners, cabins, baby sitters. *Nearby:* camping, picnicking, swimming, fishing, and all resort facilities.

Nearby attractions: George Washington Carver National Monument, Crystal Caverns, Truitt's Cave, Bluff Dwellers Cave, Lake of the Cherokee Recreation Area (Oklahoma), Arkansas Caves, Christmas City of Noel, "Prize Drive of the Ozarks," Shadow Lake, Roaring River State Park, Honey Creek Recreation Area (Oklahoma), Civil War Cave (Arkansas), Old Spanish Treasure Cave (Arkansas), Onyx Cave (Arkansas), Wonderland Cave (Arkansas).

Courtesy of Rebel Cave, Missouri.

MISSOURI

REBEL CAVE, Silva. The town of Silva does not appear on all maps. The cave is located near the junction of Routes U.S. 67 and Missouri 34, about 4 miles north of Greenville. Phone: 314-224-3242.

Rebel Cave was named for 7 men who were executed on May 28, 1865, nearly 6 weeks after General Lee's surrender. Their graves are marked in nearby Cowan Cemetery. One of these men was Rufus Holmes, grandson of Lewis Holmes, original holder of the Spanish Grant. The rebels are reputed to have hidden in the cave before their capture. Artifacts have been found in the cave, and in one place 12 inches of dripstone have formed over an ancient fireplace. Over 50 fire sites have been found in the cave, and 19 of them remain. In the photograph can be seen a huge flowstone wall that was formed at two different stages of the cave's development. Portions of the wall had to be removed to allow for the tourists' passageway.
Open April through October, dawn through dusk.
Guided tour: ½ hour.
Rates: adults, $0.75; children, 6 to 12, $0.50. Group rates available.
On premises: gift shop, picnicking. *Nearby:* restaurant, camping, motels, hotel, cabin, trailer camp.
Nearby attractions: Gad's Hill (site of a Jesse James train robbery), Stony Battery, Fort Benton, Big Spring, Wappapello and Clearwater lakes, Sam Baker State Park, Big Spring State Park.

MISSOURI

**ROUND SPRING
CAVERN,**
Round Spring. 330
yards off State
Highway 19.

Courtesy of Round Spring Cavern, Missouri.

Adjoining Round Spring State Park, Round Spring Cavern is highly decorated, and level. It is about 6,000 feet long. A stream forms dams, pools, and a waterfall. The cave was commercialized in 1930. The formations shown are known as "Stage Curtains."

Open all year, 7:00 A.M. to 5:00 P.M. daily.

Guided tour: 1½ hours.

Rates: adults, $1.25; children, $0.75.

On premises: lodge with meals to order only, cabins. *Nearby:* scattered facilities.

Nearby attractions: Round Spring State Park, Montauk State Park, Alley Spring State Park, Big Spring State Park.

Courtesy of Stark Caverns, Missouri.

MISSOURI

STARK CAVERNS, Box 129, Eldon. ¾ mile off U.S. 54 between Bagnell Dam and Eldon. Phone: 314-392-5490.

Stark Caverns has in the past produced many indications of occupancy by prehistoric man and Indians. While much exploration has been done in the cave, the end has not yet been reached, according to the owners. The small pool shown in the photo is known as the "Fountain of Youth."

Open all year, 8:00 A.M. to 6:00 P.M.

Guided tour: 45 minutes.

Rates: adults, $1.00; children 6 to 12, $0.50; under 6, free. Group rates for 8 or more.

On premises: gift shop, camping, picnicking. *Nearby:* restaurant, snack bar, motels, hotels, cabins, trailer camp, resort areas.

Nearby attractions: Lake of the Ozarks Resort Area, geographical center of continental United States, Lake of the Ozarks State Park, Jacob's Cave, Ozark Caverns, Bridal Cave, Bagnell Dam, Mystic River Cave, Bennett Springs State Park, Osage Beach, Ha Ha Tonka Castle, New National Ozark Rivers Scenic Park.

TRUITT'S CAVE, Box 34, Lanagan. At Junction of U.S. 71 and State 59. Phone: Lanagan, 417-436-2516.

An unusual feature of Truitt's Cave is a fireplace in the underground dining room. It has a natural flue and a live spring flowing out beneath it. The flue is a natural fissure in the rock, and the spring forms a pool next to the fireplace. Live trout dart about the pool. The cave was discovered in 1929 and commercialized in 1935. A large spring is 765 feet from the entrance, and visitors can drink water from a fountain installed there for that purpose.

Open all year, 6:00 A.M. to 9:00 P.M. daily.

Guided tour: 30 minutes.

Rates: adults, $1.00; children, $0.50. Group rates available.

On premises: restaurant (underground at cave entrance), snack bar, gift shop, camping, picnicking, baby sitters, motel, cabins, trailer camp.

Nearby attractions: Crystal Caverns, Lake of the Cherokee Recreation Area (Oklahoma), Christmas City of Noel, "Prize Drive of the Ozarks," Shadow Lake, Roaring River State Park, Honey Creek Recreation Area (Oklahoma), Civil War Cave (Arkansas), Old Spanish Treasure Cave (Arkansas), Onyx Cave (Arkansas), Wonderland Cave (Arkansas), Ozark Wonder Cave.

1. Big Hurricane Cave, Arkansas
2. Blanchard Springs Caverns, Arkansas
3. Buffalo River State Park, Arkansas
4. Bull Shoals Caverns, Arkansas
5. Cave City Cave, Arkansas
6. Civil War Cave, Arkansas
7. Devil's Den State Park, Arkansas
8. Diamond Cave, Arkansas
9. Mystery Cave, Arkansas
10. Mystic Cavern, Arkansas
11. Old Spanish Treasure Cave, Arkansas
12. Onyx Cave, Arkansas

13. Ozark Mystery Cave, Arkansas
14. Petit Jean State Park, Arkansas
15. Rowland Cave, Arkansas
16. Shawnee Cave, Arkansas
17. Wonderland Cave, Arkansas
18. Alabaster Caverns, Oklahoma
19. Cascade Caverns, Texas
20. Caverns of Sonora, Texas
21. Century Caverns, Texas
22. Cobb Cavern, Texas
23. Natural Bridge Caverns, Texas
24. Texas Longhorn Cavern, Texas
25. Wonder Cave, Texas

7. SOUTH CENTRAL REGION

Arkansas
Oklahoma
Texas
Louisiana

The Arkansas terrain is a continuation of the Missouri limestone country with its fine heritage of caves. Ranking second to Missouri in the number of tourist caves, this section deserves attention from those who wish to see further examples of the Ozark cave country. Going westward into the great level plain areas of Oklahoma and down into Texas, it is difficult to visualize that these areas had the climate or conditions to encourage the development of caves. A fine example of a cave in gypsum can be found in Oklahoma. Typical of Texas, the caves are usually large. One of the world's finest displays of helictites and erratics can be found in a Texas cave, hidden beneath a most unlikely, barren desert-like surface. Other caves, nearer the population centers, have fine displays of cave decoration.

ARKANSAS

BIG HURRICANE CAVE,
Route 1, Everton.
16 miles south of
Harrison off U.S. 65.
Phone:
501-439-2343.

Courtesy of Big Hurricane Cave, Arkansas.

Situated in the base of a limestone cliff, Big Hurricane Cave was used by the early settlers to protect their families during the worst hurricane ever to hit this section of the country. The cave is well decorated. Extensive zinc-mining operations in the immediate area were discontinued about 1922. The "Throne Room" is profusely decorated, as shown. The children are standing on the "throne."

Open all year from 8:00 A.M. to 6:00 P.M.

Guided tour: 45 minutes.

Rates: adults, $1.00; children 6 to 12, $0.50; under 6, free; groups, half price.

On premises: gift shop. *Nearby:* restaurant and all facilities.

Nearby attractions: Buffalo River, Buffalo River State Park, Marble Falls, Shawnee Cave, Mystic Cavern, Mystery Cave, Ozark Mystery Cave, Diamond Cave, Bull Shoals Cavern.

ARKANSAS

BLANCHARD SPRINGS CAVERNS,
U.S.D.A. Forest Service, Mountain View. 2 miles north of State Highway 14.

Blanchard Springs Caverns, Arkansas.
Photo by J. H. Schermerhorn.

Blanchard Springs Caverns, formerly Half-Mile Cave, is being developed as a tourist attraction by the United States Forest Service, Department of Agriculture. The caverns are closed to the public at present, but plans to open are under way. It is expected that first tours may begin by late 1967 or early 1968. Three tours are planned in this cave, which is 2 miles or more in length. The first Tour will be 0.7 mile, and will take 2 hours. Tour II will be 1.2 miles and take 3 hours and will feature a boat trip. Tour III will be 1.4 miles and will take 3 hours. The cave has been known since the 1800's, but Forest Service personnel first entered the cave in the 1930's. In 1955 spelunkers began exploring and mapping the cave, and in 1963 the recreational value of the caverns was realized, and work was begun. A spelunker is examining one of the many fantastic formations that will soon be available to the public when the cave is fully developed for tourists.

On premises: facilities planned include parking, Visitor Information Center with museum, and gift shop. *Nearby* (planned): restaurant, snack bar, camping, motel and cabins.

Nearby attractions: Rowland Cave, Blanchard Springs, Ozark National Forest, Ozark Mystery Cave, Mt. View Folk Culture Center, Norfolk Lake, Greers Ferry Reservoir, ranches.

Bat Cave, Buffalo River State Park, Arkansas. Photo by J. H. Schermerhorn.

ARKANSAS

BUFFALO RIVER STATE PARK, Route A, Yellville.
On State Highway 14 about 8 miles south of Yellville. Phone: 501-449-9206.

Bat Cave in Buffalo River State Park is a mile hike from park headquarters. It averages 50 feet wide, 20 feet high, and is 400 feet long. There is no lighting, nor are there walks approaching the cave. Indian Rock House is also open to visitors. *Open* all year.

Self-guided tour: 1 hour. Flashlights or other lighting required.

On premises: restaurant, gift shop, camping, trailer camp, picnicking, "Float Trips" on Buffalo River, swimming, fishing. *Nearby:* motels and other facilities in resort area.

Nearby attractions: Bull Shoals Caverns, Big Hurricane Cave, Ozark Mystery Cave, Wonderland Cave, Rowland Cave, Shawnee Cave, Old Ghost Town of Rush Creek, Lake Bull Shoals, Lake Norfolk, zinc mines.

ARKANSAS

BULL SHOALS CAVERNS,

Bull Shoals. On State Highway 178, just 4 blocks from Bull Shoals post office. (The town of Bull Shoals is not shown on many state maps. It is on Arkansas Highway 178, which runs north from U.S. 62 at Flippin.) Phone: 501-445-2101.

Bull Shoals Caverns, Arkansas. Photo by J. H. Schermerhorn.

Bull Shoals Caverns, like many others, was used by Indians as a shelter, but more recently it was lived in by Ozark mountaineers, who found the air conditioning, ample drinking water, and spring-water refrigeration all to their liking. The cave has an underground trout stream, a miniature lake, and a waterfall—all of which are seen on the tour.

Open March 1 to November 1, 8:00 A.M. to 5:00 P.M.

Guided tour: 45 minutes.

Rates: adults, $1.50; children, $0.75; groups of 20 or more, $0.75 each.

On premises: gift shop. *Nearby:* restaurant, snack bar, camping, motels, hotels, cabins, trailer camp, baby sitters.

Nearby attractions: Mountain Village of the 1890's, Top o' the Ozarks Observation Tower, Mystic Cave, Big Hurricane Cave, Shawnee Cave, Ozark Mystery Cave, Bull Shoals State Park, Lake, and Dam, resort areas.

Cave City Cave, Arkansas. Photo by J. H. Schermerhorn.

ARKANSAS

CAVE CITY CAVE, Cave City. U.S. Route 167 in Cave City.

Cave City Cave is a relatively small cave, and is composed of sandstone, as shown. After 300 feet, the cave becomes impassable because of water. The town of Cave City utilizes the underground lake as a town water supply. A motel surrounds the cave entrance.

Open all year.

Self-guided tour: lights required.

Rates: $0.25 per person.

On premises: motel. *Nearby:* most facilities.

Nearby attractions: Arkansas College, Blanchard Springs Caverns (not yet open), White River, fishing.

ARKANSAS

CIVIL WAR CAVE,
Route 3, Bentonville.
U.S. 71 and State
Highway 72 (3½
miles west of Ben-
tonville). Phone:
501-795-2277.

Courtesy of Civil War Cave, Arkansas.

Civil War Cave contains an underground lake, a plunging waterfall, as shown, rimstone pools, and a river. It was used extensively during the Civil War by General Van Dorn of the Confederate Army as a supply station and for its pure water.
Open April through November, 6:00 A.M. to 7:00 P.M. daily.
Guided tour: 30 minutes.
Rates: adults, $0.75; children, $0.25; groups of 12, $0.25.
On premises: gift shop, camping, picnicking. *Nearby:* all facilities.
Nearby attractions: Eureka Springs, Old Spanish Cave (Missouri), Wonderland Cave, Onyx Cave, Ozark Wonder Cave (Missouri), Bluff Dwellers Cave (Missouri), Truitt's Cave (Missouri), Lake Wedington Recreation Area, Pea Ridge National Military Park, Beaver Reservoir, Withrow Springs State Park, University of Arkansas, Sulphur Springs.

Devil's Den State Park photo by Phelps, Arkansas Publicity and Parks Commission.

ARKANSAS

DEVIL'S DEN STATE PARK, Route 1, West Fork. U.S. 71, then State 74 via Winslow and State 170 via West Fork. Phone: 501-846-3716.

Devil's Den State Park contains a series of caves, weird rock formations, crevices and fissures. Incredible chasms plunge to depths of 100 feet and split to a width of 50 feet, with caves zigzagging into the earth. The park has been open to the public since 1934. Visitors are shown descending into "Devil's Icebox."

Open all year, 24 hours a day.

Self-guided tours: visitors should bring their own lights.

Rates: no charge.

On premises: restaurant, snack bar, gift shop, camping, cabins, trailer camp, picnicking, bathing, fishing. Restaurant open May 1 to Labor Day. *Nearby:* nearest complete facilities in Fayetteville (20 miles).

Nearby attractions: Fort Smith National Historical Site, Lake Wedington Recreation Area, University of Arkansas, White Rock Shores Lake, Lake Fort Smith.

DIAMOND CAVE, Jasper. Off State Highway 7, about 4 miles west of Jasper. Phone: 501-446-2636.

Diamond Cave became famous in the early 1800's when a party of hunters and their dogs chased a bear into the cave. Making pine torches, the hunters followed the dogs 200 feet into the cave to an underground hallway where they found their dogs mortally wounded. Two dead bears were found, and further back a wounded bear attacked the party, extinguishing the torches. The bear was finally killed, but the story of the bear fight remains. The tour covers 2 miles.

Open all year, from 7:00 A.M. to 7:00 P.M.

Guided tour: 2 hours.

Rates: adults, $1.25; children, $0.60; groups of 10 or more, $0.85 each.

On premises: snack bar, camping, trailer camp, picnicking. *Nearby:* restaurant, gift shop, motels, hotels, cabins.

Nearby attractions: Mystic Cavern, Big Hurricane Cave, Onyx Cave, Mystery Cave, Shawnee Cave, Bull Shoals Caverns, Bull Shoals Lake, Bull Shoals State Park, Withrow Springs State Park, Table Rock Reservoir, resort areas.

MYSTERY CAVE, Route 4, Berryville. 7 miles north of Berryville on State Highway 21.

Mystery Cave was once used as a quarry from which onyx was taken for semi-precious jewelry. Since 1925 it has been operated commercially as a tourist attraction, and features an underground lake well stocked with trout.

Open May 1 through September 15 daily from 7:00 A.M. to 7:00 P.M.

Guided tour: 40 minutes.

Rates: 12 years and older, $1.00; 6 to 12 years, $0.50; under 6, free.

On premises: gift shop, picnicking. *Nearby:* restaurant, snack bar, camping, motels, hotels, cabins, trailer camp, baby sitters.

Nearby attractions: Table Rock Lake, Beaver Lake, Eureka Springs, Saunders Memorium Museum, Big Hurricane Cavern, Diamond Cave, Shawnee Cave, Mystic Cavern, Ozark Mystery Cave, Bull Shoals Caverns, Buffalo River State Park, Marble Falls.

ARKANSAS

MYSTIC CAVERN,
Marble Falls. State
Highway 7, about 7
miles south of
Harrison. Phone:
501-365-5028.

Mystic Cavern, Arkansas. Photo by J. H. Schermerhorn.

Mystic Cavern has a large natural pipe organ, in a room known as the "Music Room," from which the musical tones reverberate. The cave has large formations.
Open all year, 8:00 A.M. to 5:00 P.M.
Guided tour: 35 minutes.
Rates: adults, $1.00; children, $0.50. Group rates available.
On premises: gift shop. *Nearby:* restaurant, snack bar, camping, motels, hotels, cabins, trailer camp, picnicking.
Nearby attractions: Marble Falls, Ozarks National Forest, Diamond Cave, Big Hurricane Cave, Shawnee Cave, Bull Shoals Lake, resorts.

ARKANSAS

OLD SPANISH TREASURE CAVE, Gravette. On State
Highway 59, about 2 miles north of Gravette and 3
miles south of Sulphur Springs. Phone: 501-787-5155.

Old Spanish Treasure Cave is perhaps best known for the legends of treasure
reputed to have been buried there. It was 250 years ago that Spanish bandits from
Mexico were supposed to have buried gold statuary, several hundred bars of pure
gold, and several chests of gold coins in the cave. The cave has many small mazelike passages, and two fortunes were spent trying to locate the Mexican loot. On the
tour may be seen a little railroad that was used to remove dirt while men searched
for gold.

Open April 1 to November 1 daily from 7:00 A.M. to 6:00 P.M.

Guided tour: 30 minutes.

Rates: adults, $0.80; children, $0.30. Group rates available.

On premises: gift shop, picnicking. *Nearby:* restaurant, snack bar, camping, motel,
hotel, cabins, trailer camp.

Nearby attractions: Civil War Cave, Bluff Dwellers Cave (Missouri), Battlefield of
Pea Ridge, Lake Wedington Recreation Area, Ozark Wonder Cave (Missouri),
Wonderland Cave, Beaver Reservoir, Withrow Springs State Park, University of
Arkansas, Onyx Cave, Sulphur Springs.

Courtesy of Onyx Cave, Arkansas.

ARKANSAS

ONYX CAVE, Eureka Springs. U.S. 62 east from Eureka Springs to Onyx sign, then left 3½ miles. Phone: 501-CL3-8324 (cave booth at highway).

Onyx Cave is owned by potters who bought the cave for the excellent pottery clay it contains. The owners will demonstrate how to use the pottery wheels and coil techniques during the cave tours at no extra cost for those who are interested. The pottery factory is inside the cave. The cave itself has displays, formations, and unidentified large fossilized bones. The cave guide, by holding his flashlight behind the wall, is able to demonstrate the translucence of the formations.

Open all year, 8:00 A.M. to dusk. Later tours may be scheduled by appointment.

Guided tour: 45 minutes.

Rates: adults, $1.35; children and high school students, $0.60; under 6, free. Special family rate, $5.00 regardless of size; group rates, $0.25 each.

On premises: snack bar, gift shop, camping, picnicking, ceramic demonstrations.

Nearby: all facilities.

Nearby attractions: Christ of the Ozarks, Saunder's Gun Museum, Pea Ridge Battlefield, Beaver Dam and Lake, Withrow Springs State Park, Roaring River State Park (Missouri), Civil War Cave, Wonderland Cave, Mystery Cave, Big Hurricane Cave, Shawnee Cave, Diamond Cave, Bull Shoals Caverns, Ozark Mystery Cave, Crystal Cave (Missouri), Fairy Cave (Missouri), Marvel Cave (Missouri), Old Spanish Cave (Missouri).

ARKANSAS

OZARK MYSTERY CAVE,
Marshall. On State Highway 27, about 3½ miles southeast of Harriet. Phone: 501-448-2386.

Ozark Mystery Cave, Arkansas. Photo by J. H. Schermerhorn.

Ozark Mystery Cave has an unusual assortment of formations, some of them gigantic in size. The main first passage is 600 feet long and 100 feet wide, with a ceiling height of about 30 feet. The photograph shows the beginning of the 600-foot passage and its massive flowstone walls.

Open 8:00 A.M. to 5:00 P.M. June, July, August, and September.

Guided tour: 30 minutes.

Rates: adults, $1.00; children, $0.50.

On premises: picnicking. *Nearby:* scattered facilities.

Nearby attractions: Big Hurricane Cave, Shawnee Cave, Rowland Cave, Wonderland Cave, Buffalo River State Park, Norfolk Lake.

ARKANSAS

PETIT JEAN STATE PARK, Adona. Off State Route
10 near Adona. No phone.

Petit Jean State Park has a number of sandstone caves and rock shelters, most of which are small. There are several marked trails leading to some of the caves, but inquiry should be made for the others.
Open all year during daylight.
Rates: no charge.
On premises: camping, but other facilities unknown. *Nearby:* all facilities.
Nearby attractions: Polytechnic College, Mount Nebo State Recreation Area, Nimrod Lake, Lake Winona, Big Maumelle Lake, Arkansas River.

Rowland Cave, Arkansas. Photo by J. H. Schermerhorn.

ARKANSAS

ROWLAND CAVE, Mountain View. State Highway
14. Phone: 501-269-3217.

Rowland Cave, while operated commercially, has not been fully explored. It is a large cave, and is reputed to be connected to Blanchard Springs Caverns, which is being developed by the U.S. Forest Service. There is no confirmation of this report. As the photograph shows, there are almost no formations along a 900-foot tour.
Open May 1 to September 1, for 12 hours a day.
Guided tour: 1 hour.
Rates: adults, $1.00; children, $0.50.
On premises: picnicking. *Nearby:* all facilities.
Nearby attractions: Blanchard Springs, Blanchard Springs Caverns (not yet open), Ozark National Forest, Ozark Mystery Cave, Table Rock Lake, Beaver Lake, Eureka Springs, Saunders Memorium Museum, Big Hurricane Cave, Diamond Cave, ranches.

Shawnee Cave, Arkansas. Photo by J. H. Schermerhorn.

ARKANSAS

SHAWNEE CAVE, Bruno. 8 miles south of Yellville on State Highway 14. Phone: 501-823-7116.

Shawnee Cave was once the home of Chief Gray Wolf, whose shelter was the broad overhang of the cave entrance. A museum is housed in a 135-year-old cabin. Indian artifacts, fossils, bones, and other Early American curios can be seen in the cabin. This giant stalagmite has been formed into a column by dozens of stalactites that have become welded together like a curtain.

Open May through September from 8:00 A.M. to 6:00 P.M.

Guided tour: 45 minutes.

Rates: adults, $1.00; children, $0.50. Group rates available.

On premises: rock patios with picnic tables and chairs, museum. *Nearby:* restaurant, gift shop, camping, motels, hotel, cabins, trailer camp.

Nearby attractions: Forestry tower, Buffalo River State Park, Bull Shoals Lake, Rush Creek lead and zinc mining area, Bull Shoals Caverns, Diamond Cave, Mystery Cave, Rowland Cave, Wonderland Cave, Blanchard Springs Caverns (not open), Marvel Cave (Missouri), Fairy Cave (Missouri).

WONDERLAND CAVE, RFD 4, Bentonville. Off U.S. 71. Phone: 501-273-2919.

Wonderland Cave is part of Bella Vista Park, a 600-acre, privately owned recreation center. A nightclub is operated in the cave, complete with dance floor, orchestra, and tables.

Tours available all year during daylight hours.

Guided or self-guided tours: ½ hour to 1 hour. No lights required.

Rates: adults, $1.00; children, $0.50; groups of 25 or more, $0.50.

On premises: restaurant, gift shop, camping, cabins, trailer camp, picnicking, nightclub, swimming, pool or lake, all recreations, fishing. *Nearby:* all facilities.

Nearby attractions: Eureka Springs, Old Spanish Treasure Cave (Missouri), Onyx Cave, Civil War Cave, Ozark Wonder Cave (Missouri), Bluff Dwellers Cave (Missouri), Truitt's Cave (Missouri), Lake Wedington Recreation Area, Pea Ridge National Military Park, Beaver Reservoir, Withrow Springs State Park, University of Arkansas, Sulphur Springs.

Alabaster Caverns, Oklahoma.

OKLAHOMA

ALABASTER CAVERNS, Alabaster Caverns State Park, Freedom. On State Route 50, about 6 miles south of Freedom. Phone: 405-621-3381.

Alabaster is a form of gypsum that has been widely used for carving statuary for centuries. While gypsum is often found in caves, few caves are entirely gypsum or abalaster, such as Alabaster Caverns. Alabaster varies in color from pure white to dark grays and deep rust colors to pink. The cave stretches more than ½ a mile, with numerous passages. Here you will find some stalactites and crystals of selenite. *Open* all year from 8:00 A.M. to 5:00 P.M.

Guided tour: about 1 hour.

Rates: adults, $1.25; children 12 to 16, $0.75; 6 to 12, $0.50; group rates: adults (50 or more), $0.75; school and youth groups, $0.50.

On premises: gift shop, camping, trailer camp, picnicking. *Nearby:* most facilities within ten miles.

Nearby attractions: Chimney Rock, Boiling Springs State Park, Salt Flats, Cedar Canyon, Little Sahara Recreation Area, Northwestern State College, Fort Supply Reservoir, Cimarron River.

CASCADE CAVERNS, 1234 Basse Road, San Antonio. On Interstate 10, about 16 miles northwest of San Antonio, 5 miles east of Boerne. Phone: 512-732-2111 or 512-755-6382.

There is a legend that an early German settler lived in Cascade Caverns as a hermit some 100 years ago. There is more evidence of ancient Indians having lived there, as many artifacts have been found. The cave is about ⅓ of a mile long.

Open all year, 8:00 A.M. to 5:30 P.M.

Guided tour: 50 minutes.

Rates: adults, $1.50; children, $1.00; group rates for 15 or more.

On premises: snack bar, gift shop, Gravity House, camping, picnicking, nature trails.

Nearby: all facilities between Boerne and San Antonio.

Nearby attractions: Century Caverns, Natural Bridge Caverns, Kerrville State Park, Blanco State Park, Scenic Loop Playground, Guadaloupe Lake, Medina Lake, Bandera (a "western" city), The Alamo, Kelly Air Force Base, Lackland Air Force Base, Fort Sam Houston, Frontier Town, Our Lady of the Lake College, Landa Park, St. Mary's University, New Braunfels (old German settlement), Aquarena, Brackenbridge Park, Brackenbridge Zoo, Canyon Lake Dam.

Courtesy of Caverns of Sonora, Texas.

TEXAS

CAVERNS OF SONORA, Box 213, Sonora. 6 miles off U.S. 290 in Sonora. Phone: Sonora 2-8395.

Known since 1900 as Mayfield Cave, the caverns were kept locked until 1955, when spelunkers were allowed to enter, and made fantastic additional discoveries. So beautiful were these new sections of the cave, that it became known as Secret Cave to prevent identification and vandalism. The cave was finally commercialized in 1960 by a group of spelunkers and nearby citizens. It is without doubt one of the most beautiful caves in the country. Note the profusion of varied helictite formations pictured.

Open all year, 8:00 A.M. to 6:00 P.M.

Guided tour: 1½ hours.

Rates: adults, $2.00; children, $1.00; groups: adults, $1.50; children and students, $0.75.

On premises: sandwiches and drinks served, gift shop, camping, trailer camp, picnicking. *Nearby:* all facilities in Sonora.

Nearby attractions: Sonora, ranches.

TEXAS

CENTURY CAVERNS,
Route 2, Box 99B,
Boerne. From
Boerne on U.S. 87
(Interstate 10) turn
east 11 miles on
State 474. Phone:
512-537-4212.

Courtesy of Century Caverns, Texas.

Century Caverns has been commercialized since 1939, but was known as "The Cave-Without-a-Name" until 1963. It is expected that in the spring of 1966 boat rides will be offered into the cave, and these will cover a 2-mile round trip. The rates quoted below are for the regular trip. Visitors should inquire about rates for the boat trip when it is opened. Visitors to this beautiful cavern are asked to imagine that dinosaurs roamed the large rooms aeons ago.

Open all year, 8:00 A.M. to 6:00 P.M.

Guided tour: 45 minutes to 1 hour.

Rates: adults, $1.00; children, $0.50; group rates (10 or more): adults, $0.75; children, $0.40.

On premises: gift shop, camping, picnicking, baby sitters. *Nearby:* restaurant, motels, hotels, cabins, and other facilities in Boerne (11 miles).

Nearby attractions: Cascade Caverns, Natural Bridge Caverns, Wonder Cave, Blanco State Park, Frontier Town, Kerrville State Park, Kelly Air Force Base, The Alamo, Fort Sam Houston, Scenic Loop Playground, Guadeloupe Lake, Medina Lake, Bandera (a "western" city), Lackland Air Force Base, St. Mary's University, St. Philips College, Our Lady of the Lake College, Landa Park, Aquarena, New Braunfels (old German settlement).

179

Courtesy of Cobb Cavern, Texas.

TEXAS

COBB CAVERN, Cobb Springs Ranch, Florence. On State Highway 195 off Interstate 35 about 12 miles north of Georgetown. Phone: 512-863-3497.

Cobb Cavern is on a real working ranch on the Old Chisholm Trail. It was used by outlaws as a hideout when the Southwest was being settled. For over 100 years it was known as "Old Cobb Cave," after the original rancher in the area. In the past, Indians roamed over the territory, and many artifacts are on display at the cavern. The University of Texas has done much research in the cave, and at one time found over 30 skeletons of Indians, along with many remains of their workings. About 3 miles of the cave have been explored, and ½ mile is open to visitors. The beautiful formation pictured is called "Frozen Waterfall."

Open all year from 8:00 A.M. to 6:00 P.M. in summer, 9:00 A.M. to 5:00 P.M. in winter.

Guided tour: 45 minutes.

Rates: adults, $1.20; children, $0.60 and $0.30, depending on age; group rates, half price.

On premises: cold drinks, gift shop, camping, picnicking, baby sitters on weekends, working ranch. *Nearby* (from 8 to 14 miles): restaurant, motels, hotels, cabins, trailer camp.

Nearby attractions: Fort Hood Army Base, Stage Coach Inn and Museum, Belton Lake, Lake Travis, University of Texas, Texas Longhorn Caverns (35 miles), Lake Austin, Southwestern University, Comanche Gap, and Trading Post.

TEXAS

NATURAL BRIDGE CAVERNS,
Route 3, Box 515, San Antonio, Texas 78218. From San Antonio take 281 north, turn right at Route 1863 and follow signs. Phone: 512-438-2181.

Courtesy of Natural Bridge Caverns, Texas.

A 60-foot natural limestone slab bridge spans the amphitheater entrance to the cave. Discovered in 1960 by spelunkers from St. Mary's University, the cave was opened to the public in July of 1964. Indian spearheads, 5,000 years old; bones of extinct grizzly bears over 8,000 years old, and many other paleontological objects have been found in the cave. Natural Bridge Caverns is replete with beautiful formations, large rooms, and crystal pools. The room shown well deserves its name, "Sherwood Forest."

Open all year, 9:00 A.M. to 5:00 P.M. daily.

Guided tour: 1½ hours.

Rates: adults, $2.00; children 6 through 15, $1.50; under 6, free. Group rates available.

On premises: snack bar, gift shop, camping (planned), picnicking. *Nearby:* all facilities.

Nearby attractions: Canyon Dam, Landa Park, Aquarena, The Alamo, New Braunfels (old German settlement), San Antonio, Texas State College, Scenic Loop Playground, Devil's Backbone, Cascade Caverns, Century Caverns, Our Lady of the Lake College, St. Philip's College, Fort Sam Houston, St. Mary's University, Wonder Cave, missions, Brooks, Kelly, Randolph, and Lackland Air Force bases.

TEXAS

TEXAS LONGHORN CAVERN,
Longhorn Cavern State Park, Burnet. U.S. Highway 281 about 5 miles south of Burnet, then Park Rd. 4 miles to cave. Phone: 512-756-4680

Courtesy of Texas Longhorn Cavern, Texas.

Texas Longhorn Cavern has a human history going back to prehistoric man. Flints and other crude tools in the Cavern Museum are proof that he inhabited the cave. Later, the best Civil War spies never discovered that gunpowder was being manufactured for the Rebels in the cavern's 183-foot "Main Room." And no one has yet discovered the $2,000,000 treasure reputed to have been hidden in the cave by the notorious Texas outlaw Sam Bass, who used the cave as a hideout. The visitors in the photo are standing in the "Indian Council Room."

Open all year. April 1 through September 30: tours begin at 10:00 A.M., 11:00 A.M., 1:00 P.M., 2:00 P.M., 3:00 P.M., 4:00 P.M., and 5:00 P.M. October 1 through March 31: tours begin at 10:00 A.M., 1:00 P.M. and 3:00 P.M. daily except Sunday, when the summer-tour schedule is adhered to.

Guided tour: 2 hours.

Rates: adults, $1.50; children, $0.75. Group rates available.

On premises: restaurant, snack bar, gift shop, picnicking. *Nearby:* camping and all facilities within 12 miles.

Nearby attractions: Highland Lakes Area (many lakes and resorts with all recreational facilities), Inks Lake State Park, Buchanan Lake, Cobb Cavern.

TEXAS

WONDER CAVE
Box 167, San
Marcos. Off Inter-
state 35 in city
limits of San Marcos.
Phone: 512-392-
3760.

Courtesy of Wonder Cave, Texas.

Developed in what is known as the Balcones Fault Line, Wonder Cave has some interesting features, including the room in the picture, lighted only by ultraviolet rays which give the rocks and formations an uncanny glow and color. There is a hi-fi system that carries music throughout the cave. It has been commercialized since 1908. The cave operates Gravity House that seems to defy gravity.

Open all year, daylight to dark.

Guided tour: 45 minutes.

Rates: adults, $1.35; children, $0.80; under 6, free. Admission to Gravity House, $0.35 extra. Cave group rates: 10 persons, $0.99; children, $0.65; 25 or more persons, $0.65, adults and children.

On premises: snack bar, gift shop, camping, picnicking, Gravity House. *Nearby:* restaurant, motels, hotels, cabins.

Nearby attractions: San Marcos River, University of Texas, Aquarena, The Alamo, 7A Ranch, Austin, Highland Lakes, Natural Bridge Caverns, Lockhart State Park, Blanco State Park, Lake Austin, Baptist Academy, Southwest Texas College (alma mater of President Lyndon Johnson).

183

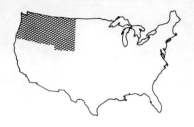

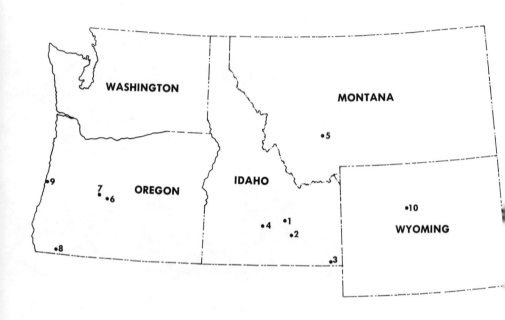

1. Craters of the Moon National Monument, Idaho
2. Crystal Ice Caves, Idaho
3. Minnetonka Cave, Idaho
4. Shoshone Indian Ice Caves, Idaho
5. Lewis and Clark Cavern State Park, Montana
6. Lava River Caves State Park, Oregon
7. Lavacicle Cave, Oregon
8. Oregon Caves National Monument, Oregon
9. Sea Lion Caves, Oregon
10. White Sulphur Spring Cave, Wyoming.

184

8. PACIFIC NORTHWEST REGION

Idaho
Montana
Oregon
Washington
Wyoming

The great Northwest, famous for its spectacular scenery and open spaces, has its share of underground wonders. The volcanic origin of most of the region precluded the formation of many limestone caves, although there are such caves in Oregon and Montana in particular. The most unusual underground features to be found in the Pacific Northwest Region are the lava tubes and volcanic caves formed in the earth-building processes that are so evident throughout the country. The rocky coasts are ideal places for the formation of sea caves, home of sea lions and sea creatures. One Oregon cave is a rookery for a herd of 600 of these beasts. Idaho has an outstanding example of an ice cave that is decorated throughout the summer with ice stalactites and draperies.

IDAHO

CRATERS OF THE MOON NATIONAL MONU-
MENT, Arco. U.S. routes 20, 26, and 93A. Phone:
208-527-3257.

Part of this 83-square-mile park is designated as the Cave Area. In the central
portion of this astonishing lava landscape, the Cave Area is reached by a half-mile
walk from Loop Drive, the 7-mile road traversing the major portion of the tourist
area. The five major caves in this area are Indian Tunnel, Boy Scout, Beauty, Sur-
prise, and Dew Drop caves. Of these Indian Tunnel is the largest, over 830 feet
long. No lanterns are necessary in this lava tube, since the tunnel ceiling has collapsed in several places. Boy Scout Cave has a floor of ice, even in summer. Lights
or lanterns are necessary in the smaller caves, which are not lighted. Signs explain
the interesting features along the trail. Close to the southernmost area is Great
Owl Cave, away from the Cave Area. The entrance is ¾ miles away from the parking area. This is a lava tube about 500 feet long, 40 feet high, and 50 feet wide. A
stairway leads into the cavern, but lights are necessary.
Open all year.
Self-guided tours: from 1 to 2 hours. Bring flashlights or lanterns.
Rates: adults, $0.50 per single adult or $1.00 per carload.
On premises: snack bar, camping, picnicking, many exhibits. *Nearby:* restaurant,
motels (18 miles east, 24 miles west).
Nearby attractions: U.S. Atomic Energy Commission Reservation, Crystal Ice Caves,
Twin Buttes Extinct Crater, Atomic City, Fish Creek Reservoir.

IDAHO

CRYSTAL ICE CAVES,

North Pleasant Valley Road, American Falls. From north, turn off Interstate 15 at Blackfoot and take State Route 39. From all other directions turn off Interstate 15W at American Falls and take State Route 39. Phone: none. Use Citizens Band Radio KFG 2300 Channel 9.

Courtesy Crystal Ice Caves, Idaho.

Crystal Ice Caves are at the north edge of the little-known Wapi lava flow. These ice caves are fissure caves occurring in the volcanic rift, and are not the more common lava tubes. They are rare and extraordinarily beautiful and spectacular. The entrance is the "King's Bowl," a greatly enlarged portion of the rift, beyond which is the realm of perpetual ice. All formations in the caves are made of ice, as shown here, instead of rock. Some formations are huge columns and stalactites. There are no steps, only trails, in the caves.

Open June 1 to November 1, 7:00 A.M. to dusk, daily.

Guided tour: 1 hour.

Rates: adults, $1.50; children 6 to 12, $0.75; under 6, free; groups of 15: adults, $1.00; children, $0.50. No advance reservations are necessary.

On premises: camping, picnicking. *Nearby:* all facilities in Pocatello or American Falls.

Nearby attractions: American Falls Dam and Reservoir, Massacre Rock, Register Rock State Park, Indian Springs, Craters of the Moon National Monument, Walcott State Park, Lake Walcott, Aberdeen Sportsmen's State Park, Snake River, Idaho State University, warm springs, bathing, fishing, boating, old Fort Hall.

IDAHO

MINNETONKA CAVE, U.S. Forest Service, Cache National Forest, Paris. 9 miles east of U.S. 89 from St. Charles. Phone: 801-945-2241.

"Minnetonka" is an Indian word meaning "falling waters," suggested by the considerable dripping in the cave. The cave is about ½ mile long and consists of 9 fairly well-defined rooms, the largest of which is about 300 feet in diameter and 90 feet high. The cave is at an elevation of 7,700 feet and remains at a cool, constant temperature of 40 degrees. Vandalism destroyed many of its beautiful formations before it was administered by the Forest Service. A scenic half-mile hike is required to reach the cave from the present parking area.
Open June 15 to Labor Day, 10:00 A.M. to 5:00 P.M. daily.
Guided tour: 1 hour. Tours leave every hour from 10:00 A.M.
Rates: $0.50 per person over 6 years of age.
On premises: no facilities, although three campgrounds are operated in Cache National Forest, the nearest a mile from the cave. Picnicking at camp grounds.
Nearby: all facilities available 15 miles away.
Nearby attractions: Cache National Forest, Bear Lake State Park, Lava Hot Springs State Park, North Beach State Park, Beaver Mountain Winter Sports Area (Utah).

SHOSHONE INDIAN ICE CAVES, Box 267, Gooding. Off U.S. 93 about 16 miles north of Shoshone. Phone: 208-934-5211.

Shoshone Indian Ice Caves is actually one cave. It is a lava tube about 3 blocks long, 30 feet wide, and 40 feet in height. Because it is a natural refrigerator, with temperatures varying between 30 and 33 degrees, warm clothing is advisable.
Open May 1 to October 15 from 7:30 A.M. to ½ hour before dusk.
Guided tour: 1 hour.
Rates: adults, $1.25; children 12 to 18, $0.75; 7 to 12, $0.50.
On premises: gift shop, 10-ton statue of Shoshone Indian Chief Washakie. *Nearby:* restaurant, snack bar, camping, picnicking. Nearest motels, 15 miles.
Nearby attractions: Sun Valley, Magic Reservoir, Shoshone Falls, Craters of the Moon National Monument (40 miles).

MONTANA

LEWIS AND CLARK CAVERN STATE PARK, Whitehall. On U.S. Route 10 about 20 miles west of Three Forks. Phone: 406-287-3771 or 3541.

Lewis and Clark Cavern is operated by the State of Montana and is the only tourist cave in the state. The cave features a novel jeep railway and a tram lift that takes visitors to the cave entrance. The tour is over a ¾-mile area, and the cave temperature is cooler than average, being 46 degrees the year round.
Open May 1 through September, 8:00 A.M. to 5:00 P.M. except June 15 to Labor Day, when it is open until 8:00 P.M.
Guided tour: 90 minutes.

Rates (including jeep and tram ride): adults, $1.00; children 6 through 12, $0.50. Group rates available.

On premises: snack bar, gift shop, camping, trailer camp, picnicking, free camping. *Nearby* (18 miles): motels, hotels, cabins, trailer camp.

Nearby attractions: Madison Lake, Missouri River Headwaters State Monument, Hot Springs, Bozeman Hot Springs, Montana School of Mines, Montana State College (Bozeman), deep copper mines.

OREGON

LAVA RIVER CAVES STATE PARK, Bend. 12 miles south of Bend. Cave entrance near U.S. 97. No phone.

A fairly small hole in the ground opens into a passageway through volcanic rocks—the entranceway to Lava River Caves. At the floor of the cave stalagmites of ice have formed, and remain throughout the year. The winding passageway develops into a tunnel much larger in some sections than the famous Holland and Lincoln tunnels under the Hudson River in New York. The cave was formed by a great bore of molten lava that was the course for a river of lava. The central mass flowed out, leaving the solidified lava tunnel walls.

Open all year, weather permitting.

Self-guided: lanterns available, for viewing cave, from park officials May through September 30, 9:00 A.M. to 4:00 P.M. Nominal charge.

Rates: no charge for cave.

On premises: picnic facilities, but no water. *Nearby:* camping facilities (Cove Palisades and Tumalo State parks).

Nearby attractions: Arnold Ice Cave, Pilot Butte, Mount Bachelor Winter Sport Area, Wickiup Reservoir, Sisters Cline Falls, Lava Cast Forest, Lavacicle Cave, Deschutes National Forest, Ochoco Reservoir, lava fields.

LAVACICLE CAVE, c/o Fort Rock District Ranger, U.S. Forest Service, Bend. In Deschutes National Forest near Bend (U.S. 20).

Lavacicle Cave is a lava cave of large extent. However, regular tours are not permitted. Arrangements can be made for an interested group to be provided with a guide, lanterns, and hard hats, which are required. These arrangements must be made in advance. In the area are about 18 other lava caves or lava tubes that can be visited, but many should be characterized as "wild" caves, not tourist caves. Most are more difficult than the average commercial cave and some extend farther than a mile. Among the easy caves are: Boyd Cave, Skeleton Cave, Arnold Ice Cave, and Charcoal Cave. Among the more difficult ones are Wind Cave, 6 or 8 unnamed caves, each having a number; South Ice Cave, Cleveland Cave, and Edison Ice Cave.

Self-guiding tours: lights required except as noted above.

Rates: no charge except for camping.

On premises: facilities not known, although camping is permitted. *Nearby:* all facilities in Bend.

Nearby attractions: Lava River Caves, Lava Cast Forest, Newberry Crater, Ochoco Reservoir, Pilot Butte.

OREGON

**OREGON CAVES
NATIONAL
MONUMENT,**
P.O. Box 7, Crater
Lake. 20 miles south-
east of Cave Junc-
tion on State Route
46. Phone: Oregon
Caves Toll Station 1.

*Courtesy of Oregon Caves
National Monument, Oregon.
National Park Service photo.*

Oregon Caves National Monument was established in July, 1909. Although long known as Oregon Caves, the phenomenon consists of a single cave. It is at a 4,000-foot elevation and has about a 48-degree temperature. Conditions are quite moist in the cave, and it may be advisable to use coveralls and rubber footwear, which can be rented from the concession. As children under 6 are not permitted in the cave, a nursery service is provided. Evening campfire programs include brief talks by National Park Service staff members of interesting phases of the monument. The stalagmites and stalactites shown are in the "Joaquin Miller Chapel."
Open all year from 8:00 A.M. to 5:00 P.M. daily.
Guided tour: 1½ hours.
Rates: adults, $1.00; children, $1.00 (children under 6 not permitted). Groups are limited to 17 persons.
On premises: restaurant (summer), snack bar, gift shop, hotel, cabins, picnicking, nursery. *Nearby:* camping, motel (summer), picnicking.
Nearby attractions: Unusual flora in and around park, Illinois River State Park, Valley of the Rogue River State Park, Grants Pass (jet-boat rides), Ben Hur-Lampman Wayside State Park.

Courtesy of Sea Lion Caves, Oregon.

OREGON

SEA LION CAVES, U.S. 1, Florence. On U.S. Highway 101, about 12 miles north of Florence. Phone: 503-547-3415.

Sea Lion Caves are sea caves in igneous rock. There is a floor area of about two acres and a vaulted dome 125 feet high. A corridor runs 1,000 feet to a sea-level opening, and a third passage enters from the north with an opening some 50 feet above the cave floor. It is the only known mainland rookery of Steller's sea lion and to a lesser extent the California sea lion. The high vault is the nesting place of many seabirds. Visitors can observe the sea lions, shown here within the cave, and other wildlife from a specially constructed platform near the floor of the cave, which is reached by elevator. From 400 to 600 of these huge mammals inhabit the waters around the cave.

Open all year from June through September, 7:00 A.M. to dusk; from October through May, 9:00 A.M. to dusk.

Guided tour: 30 minutes or more.

Rates: adults, $1.00; children, $0.40.

On premises: gift shop. *Nearby:* all facilities on Route 101.

Nearby attractions: rugged coastline, yachting, fishing. There are fifteen state parks within 30 miles of the cave, most on the coast, Winchester Bay, Tenmile Lakes, Tahkenitch Lake, Siltcoos Lake, and others.

1. Canyon de Chelly National Monument, Arizona
2. Colossal Cave, Arizona
3. Grand Canyon Caverns, Arizona
4. Montezuma Castle National Monument, Arizona
5. Navajo National Monument, Arizona
6. Sunset Crater National Monument, Arizona
7. Tonto National Monument, Arizona
8. Boyden Cave, California
9. Crystal Cave, California
10. Lake Shasta Caverns, California
11. Lava Beds National Monument, California
12. Mercer Caverns, California
13. Mitchell Caverns State Reserve, California
14. Moaning Cave, California
15. Pinnacles National Monument, California
16. Subway Cave, California
17. Cave of the Winds, Colorado
18. Mesa Verde National Park, Colorado
19. Lehman Caves National Monument, Nevada
20. Bandelier National Monument, New Mexico
21. Carlsbad Caverns, New Mexico
22. Desert Ice Box, New Mexico
23. Gila Cliff Dwellings National Monument, New Mexico
24. Timpanogos Cave, Utah

9. PACIFIC SOUTHWEST REGION

Arizona
California
Colorado
Nevada
New Mexico
Utah

This enormous area encompasses nearly all the climatic conditions of the entire country. The distances are great, and there must be many underground regions yet to be explored. There are relatively few caves for the area covered, but they are extremely varied. Carlsbad Caverns, in the lonely hill country of New Mexico, is unique in that it has perhaps the largest single room of any cave in the world. No other cave in the country can match the size and display of its massive formations. Twenty million people have gone out of their way to visit this cave since it was opened in 1924, which refutes the theory that people will not visit a natural attraction unless it is on a main road. Lava tubes in Arizona, Indian cliff dwellings in New Mexico, Arizona, and Colorado, and limestone caves in all the states make this region one of vast and varied interest.

ARIZONA

CANYON DE CHELLY NATIONAL MONUMENT,
Box 8, Chinle. In Navajo Indian Reservation from either Interstate 40 between Gallup, New Mexico, and Flagstaff or from Route 264 between Gallup and Page. Also off Route 666 between Farmington, New Mexico, and Gallup or from Route 64 west of Farmington. Phone: 602-674-5436.

Canyon de Chelly is in relatively uninhabited country except for scattered Navajo Indian homes. The sandstone canyon walls extend up to 1,000 feet from the canyon floor. The canyons contain ruins of several hundred prehistoric Indian villages, most of which were built between A.D. 350 and A.D. 1300. Many of the cliff dwellings are in caves. The best known Pueblo cliff dwellings are White House, Antelope House, and Mummy Cave Ruin. White House, in Canyon de Chelly, is in the base of a 1,000-foot cliff and is named after a long wall in the upper part of the ruin that is covered with white plaster. Antelope House, in Canyon del Muerto, is named for the colorful antelope pictures painted by a Navajo artist. Mummy Cave Ruin, in the same canyon, includes a spectacular 3-story tower house. Except for White House Trail (a self-guided mile hike in each direction), visitors must be accompanied by park rangers or authorized Indian guides at all times. General hiking is prohibited.

Open all year from 8:00 A.M. to 5:00 P.M. Guides required as above. Also, guided car-caravan tours.

Rates: no charges for entry.

On premises: restaurant, gift shop, camping, motel, picnicking. *Nearby:* no nearby facilities except trading posts.

Nearby attractions: Indian villages and homes, trading posts, Steamboat Canyon, Hopi Indian Reservation, Keams Canyon, Tsaile Lake, Wheatfields Lake, Three Turkey Ruins.

Courtesy of Colossal Cave, Arizona.

ARIZONA

COLOSSAL CAVE, Vail. Interstate 10, about 22 miles east of Tucson. Phone: Colossal Cave No. 1.

Parched bones near the entrance to Colossal Cave establish that animals once used the cave as a lair. Black smoke smudges on the walls remind visitors that Indians lived and cooked there. Deeper within the cave is evidence that outlaws once hid themselves and their loot in the cave. Although almost 6 miles have been explored, no end has yet been found in the cavern. Many attractive photographic settings, such as this one in the "Elf's Kingdom," can be found by camera enthusiasts in this cave.

Open all year, 8:00 A.M. to 6:00 P.M. Open until 7:00 P.M. on Sundays and holidays. *Guided tour:* 50 minutes.

Rates: adults, $1.50; children, $0.50. Group rates: half price for groups over 15.

On premises: snack bar, gift shop, camping, trailer camp, picnicking. *Nearby:* all facilities.

Nearby attractions: San Xavier Mission, Tucson Mountain Park, Arizona-Sonora Desert Museum, Old Tucson, Mount Lemmon, Sabino Canyon, Deer Ranch Park and Zoo, Saguaro National Monument, Madera Canyon, Pena Blanca Lake, the University of Arizona, Arizona State Museum, Arizona Pioneer Historical Society Museum, Kitt Peak National Observatory, the Papago Indian Reservation, Old Mexico.

Courtesy of Grand Canyon Caverns, Arizona.

ARIZONA

GRAND CANYON CAVERNS, Box 100, Dinosaur City. On U.S. 66, about 25 miles west of Seligman. Phone: Dinosaur 1 through Prescott, Arizona.

Grand Canyon Caverns has no connection with Grand Canyon National Park and is, in fact, roughly 120 miles from the National Park headquarters by main highway. The cave was known as Dinosaur Caverns and as Coconino Caverns. Since 1962 many improvements have been instituted, including the installation of a 21-story elevator to the cave itself and a mile-long train ride from the highway entrance to the caverns entrance building (summer only). Much of the cave is still being explored. Formerly used by the Hualapai Indians as a burial pit, many artifacts, as well as fossils, have been found. Recent finds include prehistoric human skeletons, bones of an extinct ground sloth, mummified bobcats, and marine fossils. The first stop after emerging from the elevator is at this 18,000-square foot chamber at the cavern's first level.

Open all year, 7:00 A.M. to 7:00 P.M. in summer; 8:00 A.M. to 6:00 P.M. in winter.
Guided tour: 45 minutes.
Rates: adults, $1.50; children, $0.75. Group rates available.
On premises: restaurant, gift shop, camping, motel, trailer camp, picnicking, airport, post office. *Nearby:* other facilities.
Nearby attractions: Hualapai Indian Reservation, Havasupai Canyon, Mead National Recreation Area, Dinosaur City, Hualapai Mountain Park Recreation Area.

ARIZONA

MONTEZUMA CASTLE NATIONAL MONUMENT,
Box 218, Camp Verde. State Highways 79, 279, 179. Phone: 602-567-3322.

Courtesy of Montezuma Castle National Monument, Arizona. National Park Service photo.

Montezuma Castle National Monument consists of this ancient 5-story cliff dwelling perched in a 150-foot cliff. It contains 20 rooms, and like most cliff dwellings can be reached only by ladder. In the area are other cliff dwellings and pueblo ruins. In the monument, but 7 miles away, is Montezuma Well, a huge limestone sink over 500 feet wide and containing a deep lake. Around the rim of the sink are additional cliff dwellings. Because Swallet Cave contains gases in the interior, visitors are permitted to view the ruins only from the mouth of the cave.

Open all year, 7:30 A.M. to 7:00 P.M. in summer, and 8:00 A.M. to 5:00 P.M. in winter.

Self-guided tour: approximately 45 minutes. No lights are necessary.

Rates: adults, $0.25; under 16, free. Guided tours with no size limit may be arranged with advance notification.

On premises: picnicking. *Nearby:* scattered limited facilities.

Nearby attractions: Montezuma Well, Oak Creek Canyon, Tuzigoot National Monument, Natural Bridge, Granite Dells, Walnut Canyon National Monument, Verde Hot Springs, Mormon Lake, Lowell Observatory, Coconino National Forest, Stoneman Lake, Fort Verde Museum.

ARIZONA

**NAVAJO
NATIONAL
MONUMENT**
Tonalea. Off State
Highway 64.
Phone: Tuba City,
602-283-5336.

*Courtesy of Navajo National Monument, Arizona.
National Park Service photo.*

Navajo National Monument consists of these striking remains of cliff dwellings of the Navajo Anasazi Indians. The most accessible ruin is Betatakin, a 700-year-old "apartment house," of almost 150 rooms, built on the sloping floor of a sandstone cave. The cave roof projects far out over the village. The largest cliff ruin is Keet Seel, an 11-mile horseback trip from Betatakin. It is possible but difficult to make this trip on foot. Horses can be rented from Navajo Indians through the Monument Superintendent. Visitors may view the ruins from the binocular station on Betatakin Point, but it cannot be visited without a guide. Trips to Betatakin usually start at 8:30 A.M. or 1:30 P.M. Trips to Keet Seel start at 8:00 A.M.
Open all year, 8:00 A.M. to 5:00 P.M., in summer until 6:00 P.M.
Rates: camping fees only.
Guided trips and viewing from binocular station.
On premises: gift shop, camping, picnicking. Nearest other facilities, 32 miles.
Nearby attractions: Monument Valley, Navajo Reservation, Trading Posts, White Mesa Natural Bridge, Rainbow Bridge National Monument (Utah), Inscription House Ruin, Elephants Feet.

SUNSET CRATER NATIONAL MONUMENT, Tuba Star Route, Flagstaff. About 15 miles northeast of Flagstaff on U.S. 89. Phone: Call Flagstaff operator and ask for General Communications number 774-7317.

Sunset Crater National Monument and nearby Wupatki National Monument consist largely of Indian ruins destroyed by volcanic action. In Wupatki alone there are over 800 ruins. Sunset Crater was created about 900 years ago, during the height of the volcanic activity that destroyed the Indian dwellings. The entire area is a mass of lava and cinder. At the foot of the cone is a small lava cave that contains ice the year round. Visitors are cautioned not to remove any of the ice, because removal would raise the cave temperature during the summer and cause the remaining ice to disappear.

Open all year. NOTE: Personnel on duty year round at Wupatki, from May to October at Sunset Crater. Roads to Sunset Crater are sometimes closed by snow in winter.

Self-guided tour: lights needed.

Rates: no charge.

On premises: no facilities. *Nearby:* all facilities available 10 miles away in and near Flagstaff.

Nearby attractions: Walnut Canyon National Monument, Snow Bowl Winter Sports Area, Museum of Northern Arizona, Humphrey's Peak (highest point in Arizona), Lowell Observatory, Flagstaff, Indian reservations, Lake Mary, Mormon Lake, Meteor Crater, Coconino National Forest.

Courtesy of Tonto National Monument, Arizona. National Park Service photo.

ARIZONA

TONTO NATIONAL MONUMENT, Roosevelt. On State Route 88, about 88 miles east of Phoenix. Phone: Roosevelt 4.

Three natural caves on the face of a cliff were the homes of Pueblo Indians about A.D. 1300. In these caves, they built cliff dwellings—contiguous rooms that filled the available space. They are today known as Lower Ruin, comprising 19 rooms; Lower Ruin Annex of 11 rooms; and Upper Ruin, 40 rooms. A numbered trail leads to the Lower Ruin. A trail guidebook may be picked up at the visitors' center. Numbered stakes along the trail and in the ruin correspond to paragraphs in this guide. The Lower Ruin, containing 19 rooms, shows how the buildings were constructed of unshaped native quartzite, laid with adobe mortar.

Open all year, 8:00 A.M. to dusk.

Self-guided tour: no lights necessary.

Rates: entrance fee, $0.25; children under 16, free.

On premises: picnicking, artifact collection at visitors' center. *Nearby:* food and fishing at Roosevelt.

Nearby attractions: Roosevelt Lake, Southwestern Arboretum, Saguaro Canyon and dam, Apache Lake and dam, Canyon Lake and dam, Granite Beef Dam, Tortilla Flat, Salt River Indian Reservation, Fort McDowell, Fort McDowell Indian Reservation, Phoenix, Arizona State University, copper mines.

CALIFORNIA

BOYDEN CAVE, P.O. Box 217, Kings Canyon National
Park. On State Route 180. No phone.

Boyden Cave was discovered in 1907 by a hearty logger named Put Boyden who
was trout fishing in the area when he found the dark passageway leading into the
cliff. The cave came under U.S. Forest Service protection in 1929, but first tours did
not begin until 1937, when the highway was constructed. Since 1950 the caverns
and the snack bar have been operated as a concession. A large part of the caverns are
in marble.

The drive to the cave is spectacular. The road descends from about 6,000 feet to
3,000 feet to the bottom of Kings Canyon—a curving, breath taking, awe-inspiring,
and magnificent ride. The canyon passes areas of striking granite walls spotted with
conifers up to the timber line.

Open May 20 through Labor Day

Rates: adults (12 and over) $0.45; children 3 to 12 $0.25; under 3, free.

On premises: snack bar, gift shop, picnicking. *Nearby:* Cedar Grove (camping
facilities for 2,000 people)

Nearby attractions: Giant Sequoias, Grizzly Falls, Park Ridge Lookout, Wilsonia
Village, Gorge, Horseshoe Bend, Sheep Creek Wading Area, Roaring River Falls,
Zumwalt Meadow, Grand Sentinel, Sequoia National Park, Crystal Cave, pack trips,
hiking.

Crystal Cave, Sequoia National Park, California, courtesy of National Park Service.

CALIFORNIA

CRYSTAL CAVE, Sequoia National Park, Three Rivers 93271. Take State Route 198, about 55 miles northeast of Visalia. Phone: 209-565-3323.

The cave parking area is at an elevation of 4,860 feet, about 9 miles from Giant Forest in Sequoia National Park. From the parking area a self-guiding scenic nature trail descends a half mile to the cave entrance in the bottom of the canyon of Cascade Creek near a waterfall. A good trail 1,600 feet long provides access to the most scenic parts of the cavern. Since 500 feet are retraced, the total distance traveled underground is nearly ½ mile. Those not prepared to walk for 1½ miles should not make the trip. About 30 feet inside the entrance of the cave, this wrought-iron gate resembling a huge spider web forms an effective barricade.

Open June 20 to September 12 (dates are approximate, and vary slightly from year to year).

Guided tours daily every half hour from 9:00 A.M. to 3:00 P.M. Tours take 50 minutes.

Rates: 16 years and over, $0.50; under 16, free.

On premises: no facilities at cave except parking and rest rooms. *Nearby:* nearest facilities about 20 miles.

Nearby attractions: Sequoia trees, Kings Canyon National Park, Boyden Cave, Mount Whitney (highest point in California), Tule River Indian Reservation, Lake Kaweah, Success Reservoir.

CALIFORNIA

LAKE SHASTA CAVERNS, P.O. Box 801, Redding. About 15 miles north of Redding on U.S. 99, then 2 miles on Shasta Caverns Road from O'Brien Recreational Area to the cavern's catamaran dock. Phone: 916-241-0586.

Courtesy of Lake Shasta Caverns, California.

Lake Shasta Caverns is one of the country's newest commercial caves, having been opened in 1964. Known for years to spelunkers as Baird's Cave, it was inaccessible to the touring public. Now the enterprising management has arranged for tourists to visit the cave by combining a 15-minute boat ride on scenic Shasta Lake with a ride on a specially equipped bus to carry visitors to the cave entrance more than 800 feet above the surface of the lake. Visitors may remain at the mountaintop or at the lakeside as long as they wish before or after seeing the cave. The first known visitor was James Richardson, who left his name and the date, November 3, 1878, on the cave walls. The milky white flowstone covering the fluted columns looks as if snow had been deposited on the surfaces.

Open May 15 to first Sunday in October, from 9:00 A.M. to 5:00 P.M. Off-season tours can be arranged for groups of 20 or more.

Guided tour, including boat and bus ride, 2 hours.

Rates (include round-trip boat and bus ride), adults, $2.00; children 6 to 12, $1.20; children under 6 are not permitted in the caverns.

On premises: snack bar, gift shop, picnicking. *Nearby:* all facilities, including fishing and boating in Shasta Lake resort areas.

Nearby attractions: Shasta Lake Recreation Area, Shasta Dam, resort areas, fishing, boating, swimming, Castle Crags State Park, McArthur-Burney Falls Memorial and State Park, Lassen Volcanic National Park (about 50 miles).

CALIFORNIA

LAVA BEDS NATIONAL MONUMENT, Box 865,
Tulelake. Off State Route 139, about 18 miles south
of Tulelake. Phone: Lava Beds 1.

Situated in the middle of a massive area of lava terrain, the Lava Bed Caves are among the world's finest examples of lava tubes. Here there is a series of about 19 caves that exhibit most of the lava-tube features. Sentinel Cave is so named because of the guardian figures that adorn its passageway. Catacombs Cave, one of the most striking in the whole region, derives its name from the peculiar niches in the wall resembling the burial places of ancient Rome. This cave has 1½ miles of passage. Merrill Ice Cave contains a frozen waterfall and a river of ice that remain year after year. Skull Ice Cave has three levels, and is one of the largest in height and width. Many skulls of bighorn and pronghorn were once found here. Valentine Cave contains excellent examples of varying flow levels. Other caves in the monument are: Indian Well Cave, Labyrinth Cave, Thunderbolt Cave, Golden Dome Cave, Blue Grotto, Sunshine Cave, Hercules' Leg, Hopkin's Cave, Chocolate Cave, and about five others. The caves are not lighted, but gasoline lanterns are available at headquarters.

Open all year from 8:00 A.M. to 5:00 P.M. in winter and from 8:00 A.M. to 8:00 P.M. in summer.

Self-guided tours for as many hours as desired. Bring your own lights or get lanterns (no charge) at headquarters.

Rates: no charge.

On premises: soft drinks and candy only, camping, picnicking (no water available, fires prohibited). *Nearby:* restaurant, motels, hotel, cabins, trailer camp.

Nearby attractions: Tulelake Wildlife Refuge, Glass Mountain, Burnt Lava Flow, Butte Reservoir, Lower Klamath Lake, Clear Lake, Sheepy Lake, Indian Town Lake, White Horse Reservoir, Egg Lake.

CALIFORNIA

MERCER CAVERNS,
P.O. Box 477,
Murphys. 1 mile
north of Murphys,
State Highway 4.
Phone:
209-728-2101.

Courtesy of Mercer Caverns, California.

Located in the Mother Lode country, Mercer Caverns was discovered in 1885 and was actually opened commercially in 1887. A good portion of the cave is still unexplored. The two delicate and near-transparent, crystalline, veil-like formations, called "Angels' Wings," pictured here are generally considered the most beautiful and unusual formations found within the cavern. They are over 9 feet long and 2½ feet wide.

Open weekends, holidays, and all school holidays October through May, 10:00 A.M. to 5:00 P.M. Open daily June through September, 9:00 A.M. to 6:00 P.M.

Guided tour: 30 to 40 minutes.

Rates: adults, $1.00; children, $0.50; groups of ten: adults, $0.80; children, $0.40.

On premises: gift shop and picnicking. *Nearby:* restaurant, camping (16 miles), motels, hotels, cabins, trailer camp.

Nearby attractions: Calaveras Big Trees State Park, Columbia Historic State Park, Moaning Cave, many reservoirs, Sheep Ranch, mining communities, Yosemite (60 miles).

CALIFORNIA

MITCHELL CAVERNS STATE PARK,
P.O. Box 1, Essex. 23 miles northwest of Essex and U.S. 66 (Interstate 40), east San Bernardino County. No phone.

Courtesy of Mitchell Caverns State Park, California.

Mitchell Caverns lies at an elevation of 4,300 feet in desert area and is in the middle of a state reserve noted for its cactus plants and desert wildflowers. There is a loop trail of about 1¼ miles on which Tecopa Cave is situated. The caverns were commercialized in 1932, and acquired by the state in 1956. The Chemehuevi (southern Paiute) Indians made use of Mitchell and Tecopa caverns for temporary homes long before the white man arrived in California.

Open all year, 8:00 A.M. to 5:00 P.M. daily.

Guided tour: 1½ hours. Tours conducted at 1:30 P.M. daily, Saturday and Sunday at 10:00 A.M., 1:30 P.M., and 3:00 P.M.

Rates: adults, $0.25; children 6 through 12, $0.10; groups, $0.10 each. There is a facility use fee of $0.50 per car.

On premises: camping, trailer camp, picnicking. *Nearby:* restaurant (25 miles), snack bar (25 miles), motels (65 miles), hotels (65 miles), cabins (23 miles).

Nearby attractions (more than 30 miles away but under 75 miles): Needles, Lake Mohave, Davis Dam, Fort Mohave Indian Reservation, Colorado River.

Courtesy of Moaning Cave, California.

CALIFORNIA

MOANING CAVE, P.O. Box 122, Vallecito. 2 miles
south of Vallecito on the Columbia-Sonora Road.
Phone: 209-736-2708.

There probably has been more speculation about Moaning Cave than about
any other cave in the West. As early as 1851, newspaper reports contained stories
of human skeletons being found in the cave. In fact, in 1853, the *Daily Alta Cali-
fornian* reported a find of over 300 skeletons. To this day human and animal bones
are found embedded in as much as 16½ inches of flowstone, indicating great an-
tiquity. The Santa Barbara Museum of Natural History has done much research
on these deposits. The present cave is developed at the 210-foot level, and although
exploration has been made to a depth of 450 feet, the bottom of the cavern still has
not been found. The "Capitol Dome" is but one of many unusual formations to
be found in this cave.

Open all year, 10:00 A.M to 5:30 P.M.

Guided tour: 30 minutes.

Rates: adults, $0.90; children, $0.45; 25% discount to authorized groups of 10 or
more.

On premises: picnicking. *Nearby:* restaurant, camping, motels, hotel, cabins, trailer
camp.

Nearby attractions: Columbia Historic State Park, Calaveras Big Trees State Park,
Mercer Caverns, Yosemite National Park (60 miles), many reservoirs.

CALIFORNIA

PINNACLES NATIONAL MONUMENT, Paicines. About 35 miles south of Hollister off State Highway 25. Can be reached from south through King City. Cannot be reached from U.S. 101 on west side at Soledad, except with difficulty, as there is no through road.

The caves of beautiful Pinnacles National Monument are but a small part of the scenic value of the region. Nevertheless they are of interest because they were formed by large boulders that have become wedged in narrow canyons to bridge the gorges. The caves are reached from several trails in Pinnacles of which Cave and Moses Spring Nature Trail gives the best views. All trails are self-guided and leaflets are available, keyed to the numbered stakes along the way.

Open all year—caves unlighted.

Self-guided tours: Though the trails are lighted in the cave portions, flashlights are advisable.

Rates: entrance fee, $0.25 per day per person; seasonal, $0.50 per person. New rates in effect summer of 1966. Recreation/Conservation sticker accepted.

On premises: naturalist services, hiking, picnicking, camping, evening talks on summer weekends, small museum. *Nearby:* nearest gasoline at Paicines (23 miles), no other facilities within 25 miles.

Nearby attractions: Bolado Park, Soledad Mission Ruins, Santa Lucia Memorial Park, Fremont Peak State Park, San Antonio de Padua Mission, San Juan Bautista State Historical Monument.

Courtesy of Shasta-Cascade Wonderland Association, California. Photo by Jim Martin.

CALIFORNIA

SUBWAY CAVE, Shasta-Cascade Wonderland Association, Box 151, Redding. Off State Highway 44-89, about 15 miles northeast of Manzanita Lake.

Subway Cave, a short hike from the Forest Service campgrounds, is a sinuous lava tube with several entrances, one of which is shown here. A posted map at the entrance shows the twists and turns of this unlighted and natural cave. The floor of the cave is quite rocky but not slippery.

Open all year, weather permitting.

Self-guided tour: Bring lights, for the cave is not lighted.

Rates: Cave free. Camping charges at the Forest Service, $1.00 per car per night or Conservation sticker.

On premises: picnicking, camping. *Nearby:* facilities at Manzanita Lake.

Nearby attractions: Lassen Volcanic National Park, Lake Shasta Caverns, Eagle Lake, McArthur-Burney Falls State Park, camping at Hat Creek.

COLORADO

CAVE OF THE WINDS, Box 228, Manitou Springs.
U.S. 24, about 2 miles from Manitou Springs. Phone:
303-685-5397.

The drivé past Ute Canyon to Temple Point, en route to Cave of the Winds, presents a panoramic view of Williams Canyon and the Pikes Peak Region. The return drive can be taken through Williams Canyon. Both are breathtaking routes. The well-decorated cave has a room called "Old Maid's Kitchen." Hundreds of thousands of hairpins have been left in this room in the hopeful belief that within one year they will bring the wisher a husband.
Open all year from 7:00 A.M. to 7:00 P.M. in summer, and from 9:00 A.M. to 5:00 P.M. in winter.
Rates: adults, $1.25; children, $0.75.
Guided tour: 45 minutes.
On premises: gift shop, snack bar. *Nearby:* all facilities in resort areas.
Nearby attractions: Center of resort and vacation area, Pikes Peak Region, Colorado Springs, U.S. Air Force Academy, Pikes Peak, Garden of the Gods, Royal Gorge, spectacular scenery, Eleven Mile Reservoir State Recreation Area, Cripple Creek mining town, Fort Carson, Colorado College, Will Rogers Shrine of the Sun, Cheyenne Mountain Zoo.

MESA VERDE NATIONAL PARK. Off U.S. 160, about
10 miles east of Cortez to Park entrance, then 21
miles to Park Headquarters.

The fabulous cliff dwellings in Mesa Verde National Park are dangerously weakened by time, and no entry is permitted without Park Rangers on guided trips. The area was occupied by Basketmakers from A.D. 1 to A.D. 750. From A.D. 750 until around 1100 the Developmental Pueblo Period took place, followed by the Great, or Classic, Pueblo Period from A.D. 1100 to 1300. It was the latter phase that produced the cliff dwellings in the park. The dwellings of all these groups may be seen. The largest and most famous of the cliff dwellings is Cliff Palace. Spruce Tree House is the best preserved. Others that may be seen along the ruins are Square Tower House, Sunset House, Mummy House, Oak Tree House, New Fire House, Fire Temple—an unusual ceremonial structure built in a cave—House of Many Windows, Hemenway House, and Balcony House. On the 21-mile drive to Park Headquarters are 5 numbered spots at points of interest. Theré are 2 self-guiding loops of 12 miles that can be viewed from the road. This close-up view shows details

of the construction of the cliff houses, and emphasizes their imperviousness to attack.
Open all year, 24 hours a day.

Guided and self-guided tours of varying lengths.

Rates: adults, $0.50 per day or $1.00 per year; children under 16 free. Recreation-Conservation car stickers—free entry.

On premises: restaurant (in summer), snack bar, gift shop (in summer), camping, cabins, trailer camp, picnicking, baby sitters (in summer), horseback riding (in summer), museums, restricted hiking, Spruce Tree Lodge, de luxe motel units, standard units, cabins, tents. Open May 15 to October 15 (advance reservations advisable), Morefield Village on property. Has gasoline, car service, groceries, camping supplies, showers, laundry and dry cleaning service, newsstand, curio shops, and so on. *Nearby:* all facilities at Cortex.

Nearby attractions: San Juan National Forest, Aztec Ruins (New Mexico), Chaco Canyon (New Mexico), Canyon de Chelly National Monument (Arizona), Navajo National Monument (Arizona), Hovenweep National Monument (Colorado and Utah), Cutthroat Castle National Monument, Goodman Point National Monument, Hackberry Canyon National Monument, Navajo and Ute Mountain Indian reservations.

Courtesy of Mesa Verde National Park. National Park Service Photo.

Courtesy of Lehman Caves National Monument, Nevada. National Park Service photo.

NEVADA

LEHMAN CAVES NATIONAL MONUMENT, Baker. End of State Highway 74, about 11 miles south of U.S. 6-50. Phone: Ely, Nevada, Code 702, Lehman Caves 1.

A highly decorated cave in which nearly all phases of cave development can be easily seen, Lehman Caves is noted for its unusual shield formations. Its twisting helictites grow on many formations and often cover walls and ceilings where other forms of decorations do not occur. Situated at an elevation of 7,000 feet on the eastern flank of Wheeler Peak (13,063 feet), inspiring vistas of scenic grandeur can be seen throughout the park. SPECIAL NOTE: The cave is not recommended for children under 5 years of age. The 48-degree temperature in the cave is unusually cool, owing to the altitude. Sweaters or coats and adequate footgear are suggested. The photograph shows the room known as "Cypress Swamp."

Open all year, 8:00 A.M. to 5:00 P.M. every day. Guided tours Memorial Day through Labor Day, hourly; first tour 8:00 A.M., last tour 5:00 P.M. Remainder of year, tours at 9:00 and 10:30 A.M., 12:30, 2:00, and 4:00 P.M.

Guided tour: 1½ hours.

Rates: Age 16 and over, $0.50; children under 16, free; bona fide educational groups, free.

On premises: snack bar (Easter through November 11), gift shop, picnicking, hiking. *Nearby:* restaurant, camping, motel, trailer camp.

Nearby attractions: Copper Pit (one of the largest glory holes in the mining world), Ward Mountain winter sports area, Ward Charcoal Ovens (approximately 50 miles).

NEW MEXICO

**BANDELIER
NATIONAL
MONUMENT,**
Los Alamos. State
Highway 4. Phone:
505-672-3861.

*Courtesy of Bandelier National Monument,
New Mexico. National Park Service photo.*

Bandelier National Monument is a wilderness area crossed only by trails, and covers more than 46 square miles. In beautiful canyon country, it contains many cliff ruins, such as the one pictured here, and open Pueblo Indian ruins. The most accessible of these are in Frijoles Canyon. Cliff ruins extend along the northern wall of this canyon for almost 2 miles, and many cave rooms had been gouged out of solid cliff. The best known of the cliff dwellings is Painted Cave, but a visit requires a round trip of 19 miles, hiking through rugged terrain. Ceremonial Cave requires a 2-mile round-trip hike, and is more easily visited. A 2-mile, self-guided trail can be taken in the Tsankawi Section, 11 miles north of Frijoles Canyon. On this trail are cave structures, petroglyphs, and rock carvings.

Open all year, 8:00 A.M. to 7:00 P.M. in summer, 8:00 A.M. to 5:00 P.M. in winter. *Self-guiding tours:* trails in ruins area; many back-country trails.

Rates: annual permit, $7.00; 30-day permit, $3.00 per vehicle, $1.50 per person; day use permit, $1.00 per vehicle, $0.50 per person. Educationally sponsored groups, no charge.

On premises: camping, trailer camp, picnicking all year. May 1 to September 30, restaurant, snack bar, gift shop, motel, cabins. *Nearby:* all facilities in Los Alamos or Santa Fe.

Nearby attractions: Los Alamos Scientific Laboratory Museum, Puye Cliff Ruins, Santa Fe National Forest, Rio Grande Indian Pueblos, San Juan Pueblos, Santa Clara Pueblos, San Ildefonso Pueblos, Nambe Pueblo, Tesuque Pueblo, Jemez Pueblo, Sulphur Springs, Zia Pueblo, Santa Ana Pueblo, Sandia Peak Winter Sports, Palace of the Governors Museum, New Mexico Museum of Art, missions.

Courtesy of Carlsbad Caverns, New Mexico. National Park Service photo.

NEW MEXICO

CARLSBAD CAVERNS, Carlsbad Caverns National Park, P.O. Box 1598, Carlsbad. U.S. 62 and U.S. 180 at Park Entrance (White's City), State 7 (Park Entrance Road). Phone: 505-785-2297.

Carlsbad Caverns is renowned throughout the world for its magnificence, the spaciousness of its rooms and passages, and the number, dimensions, and variety of its stalactites and stalagmites. A single room within the caverns has a floor as large as 14 football fields and a ceiling as high as a 22-story building. The large crowd of visitors in the photograph scarcely fills a small portion of this big room. Although there are many miles of passages, development has been restricted to the larger and more accessible parts of the 750- and 829-foot levels. These can be reached by a natural entrance or by elevator. At certain places along the trail, one can look down into the lower cave, which is an undeveloped section (1,100 feet). Walking distance of the complete tour is 3 miles. The most strenuous part is the first 1¾ miles, over which the trail descends 829 feet and then climbs 80 feet to the underground lunchroom. Those wishing to avoid the first part of the tour can enter the caverns by elevator and join those who have walked in as they reach the lunchroom 1¾ hours after the start of the trip. The bat flight is one of the park's greatest attractions. From April through October at dusk, incredible numbers of bats spiral upward out of the entrance and fly southward to feed for the night, returning to the cave at dawn. A park naturalist explains the bats and their flight in a talk at the entrance each evening just before the flight begins. All trips exit by elevator.

Open all year, summer 6:00 A.M. to 9:00 P.M., other times 8:00 A.M. to 5:00 P.M.

Guided tour: 3½ hours.

Rates: adults, $1.50; children under 16, free.

On premises: restaurant, underground lunchroom, gift shop, nursery, kennels.

Nearby: camping, motels, hotels. All facilities in Carlsbad and Whites City.

Nearby attractions: Carlsbad (resort), Guadalupe Peak (Texas).

Courtesy of The Desert Ice Box, New Mexico.

NEW MEXICO

THE DESERT ICE BOX, Box 12,000, Ice Caves Road, Grants. Highway 53 southwest of Grants (Zuñi-Cibola trails). Phone: none.

The Desert Ice Box is a cave in a lava flow that centuries ago turned to stone. This pictured wall of ice of unknown depths forms a semicircle at the back of the cave. At the top of the stairs leading down to the ice cave the temperature may reach 100 degrees. Seventy-five feet below, you step into a 30-degree refrigerator. Natural, perpetual ice has been insulated from the outside heat by ropy layers of lava. Near the cave old Indian trails and stone tools have been found dating back approximately 1,000 years.

Open all year weather permitting.

Self-guided or guided: natural lighting.

Rates: adults, $0.60; children under 12, $0.25; large groups, half price.

On premises: snack bar, gift shop, camping, cabins, trailer camp, motor tours, ski-run in season, picnicking. *Nearby:* scattered facilities.

Nearby attractions: Great Malpais Lava Flow, Bandera Crater, Indian Ruins, El Morro National Monument, Ramah Ruins (Zuñi Indian village), Acoma Indian Reservation, Laguna Pueblo and Mission, Chaco Canyon National Monument, Albuquerque.

NEW MEXICO

GILA CLIFF DWELLINGS NATIONAL MONUMENT,
Box 1320, Silver City. From Silver City, State routes
25 and 527 to monument. Last 4 miles unpaved, and
require normally easy water crossings. Make local inquiry for water conditions. Phone: 505-534-9344.

Gila Cliff Dwellings, like many others, flourished around 1300. There are ap-
proximately 35 rooms in the 6 caves in the monument—all naturally formed. They
were occupied by prehistoric Indians known as the Tularosa.
Open all year, 8:00 A.M. to 5:00 P.M.
Tour: about 1 hour.
Rates: no charge.
On premises: no facilities. Monument still being developed. *Nearby:* restaurant,
snack bar, gift shop, camping, cabins, trailer camp. Other facilities in Silver City.
Nearby attractions: Western New Mexico University, Silver City (40 miles).

UTAH

TIMPANOGOS CAVE,

Timpanogos Cave
National Monument,
R.F.D. Box 200,
American Fork.
State Highway 80.
Phone:
801-756-4497

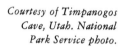

*Courtesy of Timpanogos
Cave, Utah. National
Park Service photo.*

The Timpanogos Cave system consists of 3 small caves connected by man-made tunnels. The first of these, Hansen Cave, was discovered in 1887, but the other 2 caves, Timpanogos and Middle Cave, were not discovered until 1921. To reach the cave entrance from the monument headquarters it is necessary to follow a trail that winds for 1½ miles up the steep side of Mount Timpanogos. The cave entrance is about 1,000 feet above the canyon floor, and the trail presents outstanding views of the Wasatch Mountains, Utah Valley, and American Fork Canyon. The cave is covered by a filigree of pink and white translucent crystals. Tiny pools of water reflect the beauty of the cave. This huge heart-shaped formation, known as "The Great Heart of Timpanogos," is ringed with twisting helictites and aragonite crystals.

Open May through October, 8:00 A.M. to 4:00 P.M., Memorial Day to Labor Day and until 3:00 P.M. the balance of the year.

Guided tour: 1 hour.

Rates: $0.50 per person over 16 years, free under 16 years.

On premises: snack bar, gift shop, camping, picnicking. *Nearby:* restaurant, camping, motels, hotels, trailer camp, picnicking.

Nearby attractions: Scenic Alpine Loop and the Mount Timpanogos Scenic Area, Bingham Copper Mine (world's largest open-cut mine), Temple Square, Salt Lake City, Utah Lake, Camp Floyd Historic State Park, Brigham Young University, Bridal Veil Falls, Alta Winter Sports Area, Mormon Temple, Great Salt Lake, Rockport State Park and Reservoir, Westminster College, University of Utah, Fort Douglas.

SUPPLEMENT

Available information on many of the following caves limited or received too late. Some of these caves are part of park systems where visitation of the caves is only a minor activity of the park. Many of these caves have no guide service, and often it is necessary to bring your own lights. Further local information should be obtained before entering.

ALABAMA MONTE SANO STATE PARK, on U.S. 431, about 4 miles east of Huntsville. Open April to November. A mountain park containing a cave open to the public. Self-guided, not lighted.

IDAHO CRYSTAL FALLS CAVE is 28 miles west of St. Anthony in a volcanic region containing many caves; the cave is rather difficult. Crystal Cave has a river, a frozen waterfall, and ice formations. Lights are needed for self-guidance.

FORMATION CAVE, on State Route 34, about 6 miles north of Soda Springs, is a small cave about 300 feet long which contains mineralized waters. Self-guided. Lights are advisable.

THE LAVAS, 4 miles west of Shelley, is a series of small lava caves and fissures. Self-guided, lights are not necessary.

ILLINOIS FERNE CLYFFE STATE PARK, on State Highway 37, about 17 miles south of Marion, is open all year. Two sandstone caves. Self-guided, not lighted.

GIANT CITY STATE PARK, off U.S. 51, 12 miles south of Carbondale. Open all year. Several limestone caves with evidences of early Indian occupancy were found. Park fee, $0.50. Self-guided, not lighted.

MATTHIESSEN STATE PARK NATURE AREA, on State Highway 71, about 5 miles southeast of La Salle. Open all year. Contains caves and cliffs. Self-guided, not lighted.

STARVED ROCK STATE PARK, on State Highway 71, 8 miles east of U.S. 51 near La Salle. Open all year. Contains caves, bluffs, and canyons. Self-guided, not lighted.

IOWA BACKBONE STATE PARK, State Highway 190, off State Highway 13, 55 miles north of Cedar Rapids. Open all year. Limestone bluffs along the Maquoketa River with caves and shelters. Park fee, $1.00. Cave self-guided, not lighted.

BIXBY ICE CAVE, on State Route 410, about 8 miles east of Strawberry Point; has near freezing temperatures all year. Self-guided, lights advisable.

PIKES PEAK STATE PARK, a mile south of McGregor, contains a small cave called Sand Cave, which is reached by a trail passing underneath Bridal Veil Falls. Self-guided.

WAPSIPINICON STATE PARK, on U.S. 151, about 15 miles north of Mount Vernon, contains some small caves. Self-guided.

MINNESOTA HIAWATHA CAVERNS, R.R. 2, Winona, Minnesota. Off State route 76 near Witoka south of Winona. This is a new cave opened in 1966. *Rates:* adults $1.50, children $0.75. Guided tour.

MISSOURI CRYSTAL CAVE, U.S. 65, five miles north of Springfield. Open only in summer season. Limestone cave with examples of "popcorn," "grapes" and coral formations. Open to the public since 1894, this cave has been operated by the Mann family since that time. Guided tour about 45 minutes. All facilities nearby in Springfield.

CUIVRE RIVER STATE PARK, off State Highway 147 east of Troy. A 6,000-acre park with springs and limestone caves, it is open all year. Park fee, $0.75. Self-guided, not lighted.

DOLING CITY PARK CAVE, 2600 North Campbell Avenue, Springfield. A limestone cave within the city limits of Springfield, it is open all year. There is a huge entrance arch. No charge; self-guided.

MONTANA MEDICINE ROCKS STATE PARK, on State Highway 7, about 25 miles south of Baker, contains small wind-carved caves. Self-guided.

NEW YORK SAMS POINT ICE CAVES, State Highway 52, 5 miles south of Ellenville. Open all year. A scenic spot atop the Shawangunk Mountains, it contains a series of crevices bridged over with breakdown. Ice remains until late August. Self-guided, not lighted.

JOHN BOYD THACHER STATE PARK, State Highway 157, about 10 miles west of Albany. Open all year. This park features Hailes Cavern as part of its attraction. Self-guided, not lighted.

OKLAHOMA BOILING SPRINGS STATE PARK, State Highway 34C, about 6 miles east of Woodward. A small park on the North Canadian River, it contains several alabaster caves. Open all year. Self-guided, not lighted.

ROBBERS CAVE STATE PARK, State Highway 2, about 3 miles north of Wilburton. Open all year. Robbers Cave was used by deserters during the Civil War and by outlaw gangs as a hideout. Self-guided, not lighted.

TENNESSEE CEDARS OF LEBANON STATE PARK, on State Highway 10 off U.S. 231, about 10 miles south of Lebanon. This park features the largest forest of red cedar in the country, and has several limestone caves. Self-guided, not lighted. Park fee, $1.00.

JACK DANIEL DISTILLERY, on State Highway 55, about ½ mile northeast of Lynchburg. Home of famous "sour mash sippin' whiskey," the distillery conducts tours, Mondays through Fridays from 8:00 A.M. to 3:00 P.M., through the distillery and the limestone spring cave from which the water is extracted for the whiskey.

WASHINGTON PARADISE ICE CAVES. May be seen by visitors to Mount Rainier National Park.

WISCONSIN CAVE POINT COUNTY PARK, on Cave Point Drive in Sturgeon Bay. A series of water-worn caves with small grottoes in limestone cliffs opening on picturesque views of the bay.

WYOMING SPIRIT MOUNTAIN CAVERNS, off U.S. 14, about 3 miles west of Cody. Open May to September 15 from 8:00 A.M. to 5:00 P.M. *Rates:* adults, $1.00; children, $0.50. Guided tour.

WHITE SULPHUR SPRING CAVE Thermopolis, in Hot Springs State Park on U.S. 16 and 20 in Thermopolis. *Phone:* 307-864-3848. Water trickles down from the cave to form a small pool where people can take a bath. The cave cannot be entered. Open all year, no charge.

GLOSSARY OF CAVE TERMS

In the descriptions of caves and formations, we have attempted to avoid technical words. Popular terms are used wherever possible; and we have endeavored to aid the traveler to enjoy his visit without burdening him with the chemistry and geology of the subject. The following terms have been compiled for the convenience of the reader:

ALABASTER: A form of gypsum that has been widely used for carving statuary.

ANTHODITE: A flower-like formation, usually in aragonite or calcite, forming a spray of needles from a center stalk.

ARAGONITE: A form of calcium carbonate sometimes found in caves, usually in the form of needle-like crystals.

ARTIFACTS: Articles made by man and discovered at a later date. They are usually evidence of man's previous occupancy.

BACON RIND: A thin drapery that generally forms on sloping walls; it has bands of different colors. When this formation is lighted from behind, it resembles a strip of bacon.

BEDDING PLANES: Horizontal boundaries between two adjacent layers of sedimentary rock.

BLIND CAVE FISH: Rare fish that are found in deep caves in the Ozarks and southern portions of the United States generally.

BOXWORK: Thin veins of calcite projecting from the walls and ceilings of some caves. Usually they are found in roughly rectangular patterns.

BREAKDOWN: Found in a room or passage, these irregular blocks of stone have long ago collapsed from the ceiling.

BROOMSTICKS: Tall, thin stalagmites, usually only a few inches in diameter.

CALCITE: The most common mineral found in caves, it is composed of calcium carbonate, and often takes a crystalline form, which affects the growth of the various stalactites and stalagmites found in caves.

CALCIUM CARBONATE: This mineral, $CaCO_3$, occurs in nature as calcite and aragonite, and is the principal ingredient of limestone.

CAVING: The sport of cave exploration.

COLUMN: A stalactite and stalagmite that have grown together to form a pillar that joins the floor and ceiling.

COMMERCIAL CAVES: Privately owned caves open to the public and charging admission.

CONGLOMERATE: A sedimentary rock composed mainly of cemented gravel.

CRUSTATION: Usually a thin covering of calcite or gypsum on cave walls.

CURTAIN: A thin and sometimes translucent hanging formation resembling draperies.

DOGTOOTH SPAR: Pure crystals of calcium carbonate, usually pointed, which are formed under water or in sealed chambers within the cave.

DOME PIT: A vertical enlargement of a cave corridor formed by solution, and not by breakdown, with a dome above and a pit below.

DRIPSTONE: A term used interchangeably with "flowstone" and sometimes with "stalagmite." *See* Flowstone.

FLOWSTONE: Calcite that has coated the wall or floor of a cave.

FORMATION: Here broadly used to describe any secondary growth formed in a cave, and usually composed of calcite. The term can be applied to all types of growths that appear in caves.

FOSSILS: Remains of ancient animals or vegetable matter found in the bedrock. These may be either the actual remains of the animal or a cast formed by minerals.

GEODE: A hollow nodule of stone whose cavity is lined with crystals.

HELICTITES: Twisted or erratic formations, usually of calcite, which seem to defy gravity.

KARST: A limestone region marked by sinks and caverns. Usually there are no surface streams, and the limestone has been exposed by erosion.

LAVA TUBES: Tunnels left by the draining off of molten lava in level volcanic regions.

LILY PADS: Thin, horizontal calcite formations formed at the surface of still pools.

LIMESTONE: A rock of calcium carbonate, of sedimentary origin, it is the most common stone in the formation of caves.

MATRIX: The stone that surrounds the cave: its floor, walls, and ceiling.

MOON MILK: Hydromagnesite, a mineral sometimes found in caves. It may take the appearance of cottage cheese or of a crystalline "snow."

NODULE: A small, generally rounded body usually somewhat harder than the enclosing sediment.

PALETTES: See Shields.

PECCARY: A piglike animal the remains of which are sometimes found in caves.

PENDANT: A projection of stone hanging from the walls or ceiling of a cave. It is not the result of deposition.

PETROGLYPHS: Incised drawings or diagrams made by early man on rocks and ledges.

RIMSTONE POOLS: Natural dams, formed by the deposit of calcite in slow-flowing streams, impound these calcite-fringed pools.

ROCK SHELTERS: Shallow overhangs in a cliff face that were used by early man as a temporary or permanent shelter. Popularly called caves, they usually do not penetrate into the earth beyond the reach of light.

SALTPETER MINING: An industry developed to supply nitrate for the manufacture of gunpowder. Saltpeter (or "saltpeter earth") was dug in the caves, leached in vats, and then distilled to crystals.

SELENITE: Gypsum in the shape of needles.

SHIELDS: Disk-shaped formations that project from the walls and ceilings of some caves.

SODA STRAWS: Thin stalactites just the size of the drop that has formed the "straw."

SPELEOLOGIST: A specialist in the systematic study or exploration of caves.

SPELEOTHEM: A term applied to any secondary growth formed in a cave. See Formation.

SPELUNKER: A person who explores caves as a hobby or sport.

STALACTITE: Formations of calcium carbonate that hang from the ceiling of a cave room or passage.

STALAGMITE: The companion to the stalactite formed by dripping water, usually from the stalactite above. This formation is more rounded than the stalactite, and is found on the floors and wall shelves of cave rooms.

TRAVERTINE: Calcium carbonate deposits that are alternately called "flowstone," "dripstone," or "cave onyx."

WATER TABLE: The level at which water is maintained by natural or artificial drainage from a cave.

RELATED READING

More detailed information regarding each cave listed in this book can usually be obtained from the management at the addresses listed. For further general information on caves and caving, the following list is provided. Many of these books are sold through the office of the National Speleological Society, 2318 North Kenmore Street, Arlington, Virginia.

GENERAL BOOKS ON CAVING

Bretz, J. H. *Caves of Missouri.* Missouri Division of Geological Survey and Water Resources, 1956.

Folsom, Franklin. *Exploring American Caves.* New York, Crown Publishers, Inc., 1956.

Halliday, William R. *Adventure Is Underground.* New York, Harper & Brothers, 1959 (caves of the western United States).

Lawrence, Joseph, Jr., and Roger W. Brucker. *The Caves Beyond.* New York, Wilfred Funk, Inc., 1955 (the exploration of Floyd Collins' Crystal Cave).

Mohr, Charles E., and Howard N. Sloane (eds.). *Celebrated American Caves.* New Brunswick, Rutgers University Press, 1955.

Moore, George W., and Brother G. Nicholas. *Speleology: The Study of Caves.* Boston, D. C. Heath, 1964.

Perry, C. W. *New England's Buried Treasure.* New York, Frederick Ungar, 1946 (caves of New England).

MORE SPECIFIC AND SPECIALIZED BOOKS ON CAVES

Bulletins of the National Speleological Society, 2318 North Kenmore Street, Arlington, Virginia. 27 vols., 1940 through 1965. Write for publications list.

Bailey, Vernon. *Cave Life of Kentucky,* United States Biological Survey, Vol. XIV, No. 5, 1933 (cave life in the Mammoth Cave region).

Cullingford, C. H. D. *British Caving: An Introduction to Speleology.* London, Routledge and Kegan Paul, Ltd., 1962 (a textbook of speleology).

ADDITIONAL PHOTOGRAPHS
OF AMERICAN CAVES

NEW ENGLAND AND
NORTH ATLANTIC REGION

This scene in Natural Stone Bridge and Caves, New York, shows the rushing stream entering one of the many caves there. Some of these caves have been so blocked by logs and branches brought in by the stream that entry is almost impossible. *Courtesy of Natural Stone Bridge and Caves, New York.*

A cave guide points out an attractively lighted stalagmite. For visitors to bypass this point, the entire sidewall had to be built up to the walk level, as can be seen just beneath the guide. *Courtesy of Howe Caverns, New York.*

223

Cave guides are generally well trained, and expert in answering the thousands of questions put to them by visitors. During rush and summer seasons many college students are trained to handle the added influx of visitors. *Courtesy of Crystal Cave, Pennsylvania.*

Most people associate a cave entrance with a tunnel. The variety of cave entrances is almost equal to the variety of caves. This attractive entrance to Garnet Cave, one of several caves in Natural Stone Bridge and Caves, New York, is best entered by swimming. The water is actually too shallow for scuba or "cave" diving. *Courtesy of Natural Stone Bridge and Caves, New York.*

It was perhaps millions of years ago that this huge rock came crashing down from the ceiling, forming a natural bridge over a portion of today's tourist trail. It is estimated that the rock weighs several thousand tons. *Courtesy of Crystal Cave, Pennsylvania.*

The placid lake in this cave is known as the "Strait of Gibraltar." One can visualize miniature ships passing the Rock of Gibraltar in the right center of the picture. *Courtesy of Penn's Cave, Pennsylvania.*

This "Indian Council Room" was the site of many Shoshone Indian council meetings. Here warriors beat their drums and shook their rattles and sometimes smoked their feathered pipes as they hearkened to the counsel of the chief. *Courtesy of Indian Caverns, Pennsylvania.*

MID-ATLANTIC REGION

Known as Lost John, this 2,370-year-old mummy is on display at Mammoth Cave, Kentucky, in the exact position in which he was found by cave guides in 1935. Lost John was trapped by a 6-ton rock under which he was working. He apparently loosened the rock while scraping with a clamshell for the gypsum the Indians used in making ceremonial paint. Beside him was a basket half filled with gypsum. His finger marks in the loose soil showed that he attempted to escape after the rock fell on him. *Courtesy of National Park Concessions, Inc. Photo by W. Ray Scott.*

A gallery of flowstone and stalactites. The steps were etched out of the flowstone itself. *Courtesy of Mammoth Onyx Cave, Kentucky.*

It is commonly stated that one cubic inch of flowstone is formed in about 100 years. This is by no means true, as there are too many variable factors that determine the amount of calcite to be deposited in any given time. Nevertheless, the creation of such giant stalagmites must have taken many hundreds of centuries. *Courtesy of Cumberland Caverns, Tennessee. Photo by Roy Davis.*

This mass of formations will, in years to come, fill the area so solidly that passage will be impossible. Many of the stalactites and stalagmites have already met to form columns. *Courtesy of Luray Caverns, Virginia.*

These striking pendants have created only a minute stalagmite beneath them. The stalagmites in the water were formed when there was no water in the passageway. *Courtesy of Dixie Caverns, Virginia.*

Known as "Titania's Veil," this group of draperies and flowstone is directly above the visitors' trail. The cave is full of these hanging pendants. *Courtesy of Luray Caverns, Virginia.*

The splendor of rooms such as this one must be seen to be believed. Careful placement of lighting in most commercial caves enhances the beauty of the settings. *Courtesy of Luray Caverns, Virginia.*

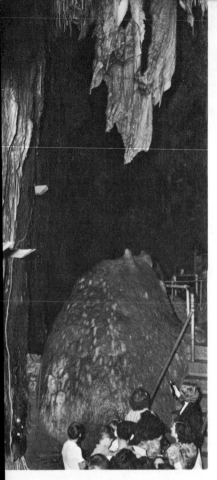

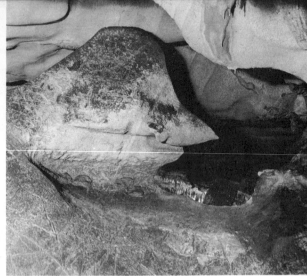

This water-eroded passage has carved weird shapes in the solid limestone. Since the recession of the water, stalactites can be seen forming on the cave ceiling. *Courtesy of Massanutten Caverns, Virginia.*

A guide points her flashlight at a stalagmite growing on a stalagmite. While men are generally employed as guides in caves, it is not unusual to find women acting in that capacity. *Courtesy of Smoke Hole Cavern, West Virginia.*

Melrose Caverns, Virginia, is known for its occupation by Rebel and Union forces during the Civil War. As a result, a large collection of Civil War relics has been housed in the museum adjoining the cave entrance. *Courtesy of Melrose Caverns, Virginia.*

Man Mountain Dean, Jr., heavyweight wrestler, is standing in water in Firemakers Cave, Florida. Dean is almost 7 feet tall, and weighs over 600 pounds. He is a permanent attraction at the cave, known as the "Home of Santa Claus" (impersonated by Dean). *Courtesy of Ocala Caverns, Florida.*

This cave has a number of colorful stalagmites cast in fanciful shapes known as "Whosababies." The cavern management claims that these are delightful creatures, shaped like people, animals, and "far-out" modernistic sculptures, yet they are natural formations. *Courtesy of Guntersville Caverns, Alabama.*

This fantastic cave entrance is 128 feet wide and 50 feet high. The thin shelf of limestone over the cave rapidly thickens as it approaches the hill in back of the cave. Though it might seem that the thin limestone could scarcely bear the weight of the people standing on top, it actually can support hundreds of tons. The entire roof of the huge entrance room is a solid slab of smooth limestone. *Courtesy of Cathedral Caverns, Alabama.*

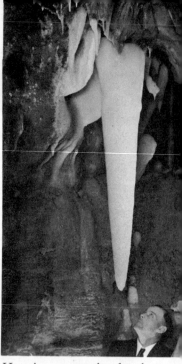

Evidences of vandalism can be seen on this beautiful formation. Apparently Indians had more respect for the beauties of our caverns than our present-day visitors, as it is rare to find any evidence of Indian damage in caves. The commercialization of so many caves has helped to eliminate their destruction and to preserve them for future generations. *Courtesy of Lost River Cave, Wisconsin.*

Here is an example of a classic stalactite formation. This white formation grew from small stalactites like those at the top of the picture. An easy way to remember the difference between a stalactite and a stalagmite is that stalaCtites (with a "C") grow from the ceiling, and stalaGmites (with a "G") grow from the ground. *Courtesy of Ohio Caverns, Ohio.*

Few caves exhibit the perfection of these pure white calcite formations. Their shiny whiteness, in sharp contrast to the rust-colored mud and limestone, makes them appear almost unreal and unnatural. *Courtesy of Ohio Caverns, Ohio.*

Many underground streams of water seemed to come from nowhere in the area of Spook Cave, Iowa. In one particular spot there was always a weird sound emanating from underground. By blasting and digging, the underground river, seen here, was found to be the source of the eerie noises, and Spook Cave was discovered. *Courtesy of Spook Cave, Iowa.*

Banks of flowstone are created by water dripping on walls, floors, and ledges of caverns. In time an entire cave can be filled with such flowstone, making entry impossible. *Courtesy of Niagara Cave, Minnesota.*

This perfectly shaped, glistening formation is of Galena limestone. Galena limestone was formed 350 million years ago, and this creation of nature is believed to be hundreds of thousands of years old. *Courtesy of Wonder Cave, Iowa.*

This "keyhole" passage is typical of many water-worn cave passages that sometimes run for many miles. *Courtesy of Niagara Cave, Minnesota.*

It was on this very spot that Jesse James was reputed to have "holed up" for 3 days after robbing the Northfield Bank. The fine silt and dust were created by the passage of tourists through this sandstone cave, since sandstone erodes easily. *Courtesy of Robber's Cave, Nebraska.*

Dogtooth spar crystals are not found in many caves. The caves in South Dakota have more of this type of crystal than any other cave area. These fine examples are from Jewel Cave National Monument, South Dakota. *Courtesy of Jewel Cave National Monument. National Park Service Photo.*

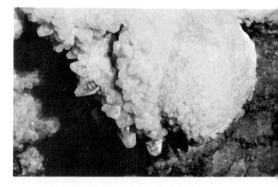

Spelunkers admiring the formations in a newly discovered passage. Tourists always get a better view of a cave than spelunkers, whose vision is limited by the relatively dismal lighting of the carbide lamps on their helmets. *Courtesy of Rushmore Cave, South Dakota.*

The full effect of the height of the huge entrance room in Marvel Cave is lost in photography. Actually, the cave entrance is 204 feet above the spot from which the photograph was taken. This is about the equivalent of a 22-story building. The room is 225 feet wide and 411 feet long. The benches face the auditorium and dance floor. *Courtesy of Marvel Cave, Missouri.*

This couple is entranced by watching dancing fairies or elves in beautiful Fairy Cave, Missouri. *Courtesy of Fairy Cave, Missouri. Photo by Walker—Missouri Commerce.*

Hundreds of couples square dance on especially constructed platforms, and scores of spectators are seated on bleachers, all beneath the great natural dome in Marvel Cave's yawning "Cathedral Room." *Courtesy of Marvel Cave, Missouri.*

A mass of "soda-straw" and "carrot" stalactites have formed on the ceiling. Most of the carrot formations are suspended from a ¼-inch soda straw that will break off at the slightest touch. *Courtesy of Meramec Caverns, Missouri.*

Like a magnificent stage curtain, this perfect formation glistens and sparkles under 62 different lighting effects used to illuminate its majestic splendor. This beauty is 70 feet high, 60 feet wide, and 35 feet thick, and must have taken untold millions of years to form. *Courtesy of Meremec Caverns, Missouri.*

Some call them "elephant ears"; others call them "hanging tobacco leaves," but by whatever name they are called these beautiful translucent crystalline draperies are found here in profusion. Lights placed behind the draperies cause the formations to shine a glowing orange-red. *Courtesy of Marvel Cave, Missouri.*

Stalagmites such as this huge one are usually formed by the drippings from a stalactite. This huge formation, 55 feet in overall height and 126 feet in circumference, has no stalactite above it. *Courtesy of Marvel Cave, Missouri.*

The magnificent "Castle of the White Giants" is guarded by a series of rimstone pools that can be seen in the foreground of this scene. *Courtesy of Natural Bridge Caverns, Texas.*

These massive formations are called the "King's Throne." Huge stalagmites generally sparkle like diamonds as a result of the faceted crystals in their structure. *Courtesy of Natural Bridge Caverns, Texas.*

Onyx breakdown from the ceiling takes the shape of a sea monster rising out of the depths. *Courtesy of Onyx Cave, Arkansas.*

235

These fabulous helictites grow in defiance of all laws of gravity. The stalactites in the upper left of the photo have drops of water on the tips of the formations. Such drops also appear in the cluster of helictites. These are as brittle as china, and will snap off at the slightest pressure. Portions of Sonora Caverns were so filled with formations that it was impossible to go farther into the cave without breaking a small path through them. *Courtesy of Caverns of Sonora, Texas.*

A spelunker examining delicate "soda straws" 4 to 5 feet long. Soda straws, which are true stalactites, rarely grow longer than 8 to 10 inches, since the hole in the center through which the water drips generally becomes clogged, forming a more conventional type of stalagmite. The slightest touch will break these off. On the left can be seen unusual helictites. *Courtesy of Caverns of Sonora, Texas.*

PACIFIC NORTHWEST REGION

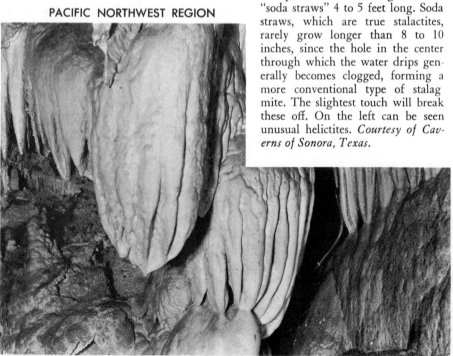

Oregon Caves, Oregon, known as the "Marble Halls of Oregon," has clusters of banana-like bunches in what is called "Banana Grove." Some of the bunches are 4 to 5 feet tall. *Courtesy of Oregon Caves National Monument. National Park Service Photo.*

A simulation of early western settlers searching for stolen loot left by outlaws in Colossal Cave, Arizona. In this cave, as in many others, robbers were reputed to have hidden or buried their loot in a secret chamber. None has ever been recovered. *Courtesy of Colossal Cave, Arizona.*

Known as the "Parachutes," these magnificent shields are the "trademark" of Lehman Caves National Monument, Nevada. It should be noted that true shields are not necessarily attached to the ceilings. Often there is a 5- or 6-foot space between most of the top of the palette and the ceiling. *Courtesy of Lehman Caves National Monument. National Park Service Photo.*

INDEX

Names preceded by an asterisk (*) and *without a page number* are caves that are believed to be closed.

Names preceded by an asterisk (*) and *with a page number* are names of caves not presently in use. The proper cave name will be found on the page indicated.

Page numbers in italics refer to illustrations.

The index does not include names listed in the cave descriptions under "Nearby Attractions."

Names in quotations are the names given to formations or scenes in caves.

243